Fat

| THE ANTHROPOLOGY |
| OF AN OBSESSION |

Edited by Don Kulick and Anne Meneley

Jeremy P. Tarcher/Penguin
a member of Penguin Group (USA) Inc.
New York

JEREMY P. TARCHER/PENGUIN
Published by the Penguin Group
www.penguin.com
Penguin Group (USA) Inc., 375 Hudson Street, New York, New York 10014, USA •
Penguin Group (Canada), 10 Alcorn Avenue, Toronto, Ontario, Canada M4V 3B2
(a division of Pearson Penguin Canada Inc.) • Penguin Books Ltd, 80 Strand, London
WC2R 0RL, England • Penguin Ireland, 25 St Stephen's Green, Dublin 2, Ireland
(a division of Penguin Books Ltd) • Penguin Group (Australia), 250 Camberwell Road,
Camberwell, Victoria 3124, Australia (a division of Pearson Australia Group Pty Ltd) •
Penguin Books India Pvt Ltd, 11 Community Centre, Panchsheel Park, New Delhi–110 017,
India • Penguin Group (NZ), Cnr Airborne and Rosedale Roads, Albany, Auckland 1310,
New Zealand (a division of Pearson New Zealand Ltd) • Penguin Books (South Africa)
(Pty) Ltd, 24 Sturdee Avenue, Rosebank, Johannesburg 2196, South Africa

Penguin Books Ltd, Registered Offices: 80 Strand, London WC2R 0RL, England

Most Tarcher/Penguin books are available at special quantity discounts for bulk purchase
for sales promotions, premiums, fund-raising, and educational needs. Special books or
book excerpts also can be created to fit specific needs. For details, write Penguin Group
(USA) Inc. Special Markets, 375 Hudson Street, New York, NY 10014.

Library of Congress Cataloging-in-Publication Data

Fat : the anthropology of an obsession/edited by Don Kulick and Anne Meneley.
p.   cm.
Includes bibliographical references.
ISBN 1-58542-386-6
1. Obesity—Social aspects.   2. Medical anthropology.   I. Kulick, Don.   II. Meneley, Anne.
RC628.F33   2005   2004055366
616.3'98—dc22

Printed in the United States of America
3   5   7   9   10   8   6   4   2

This book is printed on acid-free paper. ∞

Book design by Ellen M. Lucaire

FOR C. J. STROUD
AND THEO BANELIS

CONTENTS

Fat

Introduction

This book is about a subject that leaves few people unmoved. It is about a phenomenon that conjures images of repulsion, disgust, and anxiety for some, but associations of comfort, delight, and beauty for others. We are talking, of course, about "fat."

Fat is a three-letter word larded with meaning. Those meanings are complex; fat means a lot of different things to a lot of different people. It can refer to a substance or a food. It can be a description of someone's body. It can be an allusion to something good ("the fat of the land"), or something bad ("fat chance").

In many parts of the world, fat foods and fat bodies are the provenance of the rich; in contemporary North America and Europe, they have become symbolic of the poor.

Indeed, in contemporary North America and Europe, the tone with which the word *fat* is uttered is often concerned, ashamed, alarmist, or condemnatory. Fat, we are told relentlessly, is bad. Say the word *fat* out loud in public and you will likely get a reaction. Anyone overhearing you may look away, cringing from what they may hear as a searing appraisal of their own physique. Or they might look around, curious to spot the fattie you must have in sight. Or they might look right at you, shushing you as if it were impolite to even mention the word in public. What most people hearing *fat* probably would *not* feel is indifferent. Allyson Mitchell's chapter in this book ("Pissed Off," page 211) describes a fat activist gathering, where more than a dozen fat women stood on a sidewalk and asked passersby, "Do you think I'm fat?" The passersby were dumbfounded. That a fat woman would actually *invite* someone to call her fat seemed unimaginable. It had to be some kind of trap (as, indeed, it was: regardless of what answer people managed to squeak out, they were handed a fat-affirmative flyer).

There are good reasons why people might think that fat warrants concern. A recent special report on obesity in *The Economist* summed up some of the problems: "Although being fat does not necessarily kill you, it increases the risk that you will suffer from nasty diseases and die early. Women who are just overweight have a risk five times higher than the average of developing type-2 diabetes. Women who are severely obese have a risk more than 50 times higher. Obesity is implicated in cancer: a recent study in America showed that 14 percent of cancer deaths in men and

20 percent in women could be attributed to it. And being overweight is one of the main causes of heart disease, the world's biggest cause of death, above wars, malaria, AIDS, or any of the other more spectacular killers."[1]

The *Economist* report would seem to brook no dissent. Faced with this kind of incontrovertible evidence (which we are all force-fed, in various forms, every day), how can people possibly allow themselves to get fat?

Maybe because real life is complicated.

In 1996, Richard Klein, a professor of French at Cornell University, and a self-identified fat man, wrote a crisp little book called *Eat Fat*. The book's title is partly a challenge, a cheeky imperative that dares us to think critically about why we feel we have to justify the pleasure we experience when we bite into a doughnut or lick our fingers after polishing off a barbecued sparerib.

But *Eat Fat* is also an ironic comment on the state of the world. Klein points out that one of the main reasons why the fat we eat tends to be flavored with guilt is that for more than fifty years the health-beauty-fitness industry has mobilized immense creative and financial resources to persuade us of the virtues of being skinny. Consumers spend billions of dollars a year on books, videos, dieting programs, drugs, fitness club memberships—all in an effort to lose weight. In addition, we spend billions more on "lite" or "low-fat" food. With this amount of money and time spent dieting, getting fit, and eating "lite," one might expect that the world was getting thinner. In fact, of course, the opposite is happening.

People worldwide are getting fatter, not only in the industrialized countries, but also in an increasing number of developing nations, such as Samoa, where a whopping 75 percent of the urban population is now obese. Obesity has reached "epidemic proportions": the World Health Organization (WHO) says that of an estimated one billion overweight adults in the world, at least 300 million of them are obese. WHO has begun using the term *globesity* to designate the increasing spread of fat around the globe. Globesity is tied to the fact that more and more people are moving to cities, eating ever-increasing quantities of high-fat, calorie-dense junk food, and living sedentary lives. In industrialized countries, increasing rates of obesity are also related to the fact that diets just don't work: 76 percent of dieters are fatter three years after beginning a diet than they were when they began. After five years the number jumps to a staggering 95 percent.[2] In the U.S., the consumption of fat and the consumption of "lite" or "low-fat" foods are increasing simultaneously. In other words, people are eating more fat, but they are also buying other, low-fat foods, to make them feel less guilty about eating the fat. And then they eat those too.

Richard Klein suggests that since dieting and buying memberships in health clubs only seems to be making us fatter, maybe eating fat would make us thin. It would, he says, at least make us less neurotic.

Perhaps. But when you think about fat, it is important to know that not everybody is neurotic about it. Or at least not neurotic in the same way. Definitions of fat, and opinions about its value, are anything but simple.

This book about fat is rather different from most other books on the topic. It takes no position on dieting. It points no fingers. It preaches no message. Instead, *Fat* explores the many dimensions of fat: fat as substance, as food, a condition, a language, an aesthetic, and even as a matrix of erotic possibility.

The authors are thirteen professional anthropologists and a fat activist. That a fat activist might have something interesting and relevant to say about fat is obvious. What thirteen anthropologists might have to say about it is perhaps slightly more mysterious.

Anthropologists study human cultures. We do so by conducting fieldwork, which consists of living among the people we want to know about for extended periods—usually at least a year. The idea behind fieldwork is that if we observe and talk to people over a long period of time, in a wide range of contexts, then we will be in a better position to understand what they do and why they do it than we would if we just interviewed them briefly or asked them to fill out a questionnaire.

Anthropology emerged as a discipline in the late nineteenth century as the study of non-Western people. It is still associated in the popular imagination with the study of African tribes or South Sea islanders. A main reason for this is that the quintessential anthropologist in the minds of many is the great American anthropologist Margaret Mead. Mead was an international celebrity during her lifetime. She conducted fieldwork in exotic places like Samoa, New Guinea, and Bali, and she used her knowledge about those places to explain to Americans that their way of thinking about seemingly self-evident things—like gender, or adolescence, or sexuality—were not the only ways, nor were they necessarily the best, the most humane, or the most reasonable ways in the world. Mead's goal was to make the strange comprehensible and familiar. But she also wanted to make the familiar strange.

Anthropologists still work in non-Western societies. We have ourselves conducted fieldwork in Papua New Guinea (Don) and

Yemen (Anne), and we have written books about the people we came to know in those places. But, like many other anthropologists, we have also done fieldwork in places like Sweden and Italy—not exactly the kinds of sites that most people most likely think of when they hear the word *anthropology*.

In fact though, anthropological fieldwork today is conducted everywhere. There is nothing about anthropological methods, or the way anthropologists try to explain human culture, that limits it to non-Western or small-scale societies or to particular topics. Anthropology today is conducted from the deserts of Niger to yuppie coffee cafés in the United States.

When thirteen anthropologists, each with experiences of working in societies from all over the world, turn their attentions to fat, the results are surprising, illuminating, and entertaining. By putting fat in a broad, cross-cultural perspective, they show us that, around the world and even in unexpected quarters in the United States, fat is anything but the straightforwardly bad thing that it is usually presented as being. To the contrary: fat is often a positively valued substance. It can be lovingly cherished olive oil. It can symbolize belonging, in the form of Spam. It can evoke nostalgia for the good old days, as thinly sliced lard. Or it can be savored as a naughty moment of indulgence when, like whipped cream, it is spritzed on top of a cup of coffee.

Fat bodies, too, are not always stigmatized. There are places like Niger, in Africa, where they are considered sexy and ideal. There are other places, like the Andes Mountains, where they symbolize strength and health—attractive qualities that make them desirable targets for the dreaded *pishtaco*, a kind of vampire who sucks not blood but fat. There are cultures like hip-hop, or pornography, where fat bodies are objects of adulation. There are other contexts, like the theatrical performances of fat activists, where fat bodies are displayed, valorized, and politicized. And there circumstances, such as the medical condition called lipodystrophy, where the fat in a person's body drains away and redistributes itself, and where sufferers long for that fat and mourn its loss.

Of course, the opposite is also true. In Sweden, there are teenage girls who abhor fat and talk endlessly about how they can avoid it or shed it. In Portugal, there are women who are regarded as living saints because they never eat. In Brazil, there are women who spend substantial sums of money on pills that they say make them leak fat.

By collecting together in one anthology such a broad range of meanings and perceptions of fat, and by compiling a catalog of such diverse feelings about it, we want to show that there are no obvious or natural or universal responses to fat. Fat is a substance; it is tangible and physical, to be sure. It exists in food, and it accumulates on bodies. But it isn't just a chemical or biological fact. It is also a supremely cultural fact.

Mark Graham coins the term *lipoliteracy* in his chapter, "Chaos" (page 169), to refer to the way that we all "read" fat: that is, the way we see fat or the absence of fat as conveying a message, as telling us something good or bad about food, bodies, and people. Lipoliteracy can also refer to the act of learning about fat by reading about it. This double entendre is the spirit in which we offer *Fat*: as a book that contributes to the literature *on* fat, and to people's "readings" *of* fat. Our hope is that reading this book will complicate and enhance your own readings of fat. *Fat* should make those readings richer, more nuanced, more open—and more fun. Like Richard Klein's message with his book about fat, our goal can also be summed up in two little words. Remember that Klein wanted us all to *Eat Fat*. Well, we think the many dimensions of fat deserve far more intelligent thought than they normally receive—even in a world that sometimes seems to talk about little else but fat. So whether or not you actually do *eat fat*, we hope this book will stimulate you, now and in the future, to *think fat*.

Don Kulick and Anne Meneley
Stockholm and Toronto
June 2004

 Ideal

Rebecca Popenoe

What would it feel like to suddenly find oneself in a place where women strive to be as fat as possible? Would it be liberating? Would it be easier to love one's body? Or would the same issues and pressures around eating and the body still arise, except in reverse?

I lived for four years in just such a place, among desert Arabs in Niger, a country that borders Nigeria in the south and Algeria in the north. Living in tents and simple adobe houses in the sparsely inhabited reaches of the southern Sahara, these Arabs have for centuries cultivated an ideal of what Westerners would consider obesity in women, and girls are force-fed in order to achieve this ideal. In my work with these people, I quickly learned that even in the absence of glossy magazine pictures of fashion models, or any images of what women "should" look like besides the real-life women around them, body ideals are still very important. Intriguingly, however, attempting to achieve the fat body ideal did not seem to create the same feelings of personal anguish for these Arab women that striving for the thin body ideal seems to for many women in the West. As I learned to see the world through their eyes, I also discovered that changing the way I looked at the body was one of the hardest cultural leaps I, as an anthropologist and as a woman, have ever had to make.

Stepping on the Scale in Niger

I first came to this western corner of Niger in the mid-1980s as a Peace Corps volunteer posted to a village at a Saharan crossroads. I worked at the local clinic alongside local Nigerien nurses, weighing and measuring children and helping to treat, ironically, undernourished children. I soon discovered that women from all the diverse ethnic groups in the area wanted to be fat: Hausa, Zarma, Fulani, Tuareg, and the local Arabs. The Nigerien nurses I worked with, who were mostly from villages, would occasionally weigh themselves, just like women in the West might do when they find themselves in the vicinity of a scale. Unlike women in the West, however, who learn at an early age to remove shoes and as much clothing as possible before stepping on the scale for its verdict, the Nigerien nurses always put clothes *on*. They nonchalantly picked up their shawls, sweaters, and any other loose items of clothing they had with them before stepping on the scale. Taking their shoes off to weigh themselves was out of the question, because this would subvert their goal, which was to weigh as much as possible.

Weighing oneself was probably a relatively recently learned behavior for these women, a new practice made possible by the clinic scale. But for them, as for women of all ethnic groups in Niger and indeed in much of Africa, the hope is always that one will be bigger, not smaller. Among the seminomadic Arabs of the region, who had long had slaves and who now hired servants to do much of the hard labor, the ideal of fatness was almost a raison d'etre for women.

Nigerien Arabs and the Fat Female Ideal

One hot, still afternoon partway through my Peace Corps stay, I stumbled into a compound where an Arab girl sat alone on a mat, disconsolately stirring an oversize bowl of porridge with a similarly oversize ladle. A woman nearby spoke harsh words to her, urging her to drink up the porridge. It dawned on me that the unwieldy bodies of the village Arab women, extreme even among peoples whose women all strived for wide girth, was achieved through the more or less forced consumption of food in childhood. Soon I learned from my Arab friend Boukia that she had indeed undergone this fattening process as a child, which had endowed her with what she called the "beautiful" stretch marks on her arms. Boukia did not have the means now to properly fatten her own daughters, but she told me she would do so if she had access to the necessary quantities of millet and milk.

I left Niger after two years, when my Peace Corps work was

over. But I went back again in the early 1990s and moved to a pre-dominantly Arab village to study the bodily ambitions of Nigerien Arabs in more depth.[1] By hunting down information in old missionary and travelers' accounts, I had learned that a number of African peoples have had traditions of secluding girls before marriage and fattening them. However, the Nigerien Arabs and Mauritanian Moors to whom they are related seem to be the only ethnic group on record that begins fattening girls in early childhood. Historical accounts suggest that the practice has been going on for centuries across a wide swath of the western and central Sahara.

In the more remote village where I now established my strange Western presence, women were wonderfully welcoming, though it made little sense to them that, given their illustrious history and Muslim piousness, I'd want to ask questions about something as banal as fattening. Since a number of girls were being quietly fattened in corners of their tents, however, I soon learned the basic facts of the practice. Under the close watch of a female relative, girls begin ingesting large quantities of milk and porridge every day, starting when they lose their first teeth and continuing until they reach adolescence. The pudginess they develop is thought to (and, according to biologists, probably does) hasten the onset of puberty and the possibility of childbearing. Ideally, girls in this society are married in early adolescence. By then, women told me, girls have "learned the value of fatness themselves" and maintain their fatness on their own throughout their adult lives by stuffing themselves with a kind of dry, homemade couscous thought to maintain fleshiness in more mature women. Yet the women seemed reluctant to talk about this, and I soon learned why. To talk a lot about fattening was to risk casting the evil eye on the young girls whose central purpose in life at this stage was to make their blossoming young bodies sexually attractive and beautiful. Even if one did not consciously mean to cause ill, commenting on a girl's fat could indicate envy and, according to local theories of health and morality, cause the girl to lose weight or become sick.

The risk that anyone would cast the evil eye on me, however, was minimal. My own bodily charms, meager as they were in my own country, certainly meant even less in this Saharan world. At home, where I flattered myself that my subtly visible collarbones were an ideal element of a young female body, in the eyes of the people I was living with, these bony protrusions brought to mind only unflattering images of scrawny cows! They coveted instead a smooth chest with no hint of collarbones and a long neck on which to display gold and bead necklaces. Since women who have their veils up to cover their hair and body may still show their face and neck, there is particular attention paid to making this area beautiful. When I would return to the village from brief trips to Niger's capital, Niamey, "fattened" there on Western foods I longed for after long stretches of the desert diet, the women would all comment appreciatively that my collarbones were not quite so noticeable. They were attuned to every pound I would lose or gain, far beyond even my own awareness.

These Nigerien Arab women spent as much time as possible sitting or lying down, letting servants do the work of carrying water and cooking. But whenever they did raise themselves, they took the opportunity to show their large bodies off to advantage. Walking as slowly as they could, they swayed their buttocks from side to side, emphasizing this most important feature of a woman's charms. Once, a young man who worked for one of the families I spent time with sent all the women present into peals of laughter imitating this walk, wildly poking his butt out from side to side as he tripped across the sandy yard. In one of the many seeming contradictions of this Muslim society of veiled women, men told me they could readily identify any woman at a distance from her walk and her silhouette. The veil that conceals is just as important for what it reveals.

I was considered so skinny that the Niger women I lived with did not, in fact, consider me fully a woman. "Why don't you marry Ahmed?" they said, referring to a sixteen-year-old boy, alerting me to the fact that even though I was in my late twenties, without a suitably rotund body I was essentially a young girl in their eyes. With what they considered my sticklike body, I was clearly abnormal. I think that my hosts' distaste for my thinness made living alone in their midst easier: Certainly no man would really want me, and so I was not a threat to the women in any way.

So important are big buttocks to femininity in Niger that the simple dolls girls make out of clay often have no arms or legs but do have clearly demarcated buttocks. A woman, like these dolls, should ideally not have to labor, walk, or really move at all. By contrast, male dolls—and men themselves, it often seemed—were all arms and legs. The male dolls were merely two crossed sticks with a piece of cloth thrown over them. It is an apt representation, as Nigerien Arab men tend to be thin and wiry, constantly on the move.

It was not easy for me to learn to appreciate the Nigerien love of stretch marks. Stretch marks are sung about glowingly in a love song as a "waist lined with stripes," and all young women hope to acquire them on their legs and arms, as well. "Anyone can get stretch marks on their stomachs," women told me, but stretch marks on your arms and legs are a real achievement. When my friend Boukia made me a cloth doll to take home with me, she stitched a scrap of striped cloth across the doll's stomach, thereby mimicking the vaunted stretch marks.

When I asked people in the village whether the extreme fat body ideal was perhaps on the wane, both men and women told me that they no longer liked very fat women as they used to in the old days.[2] But when I asked them to name a woman who they thought was beautiful, they inevitably mentioned the very fattest women in the community. And although in less remote areas of West Africa, where Western values and images have made inroads, Western body ideals are contending with fatter traditional ones, the Nigerien Arab women I knew never believed my seemingly self-serving claims that women where I came from wanted to be as thin as possible. They cited an apparently pleasingly plump French nurse with the organization Doctors Without Borders who had once passed through town as clear evidence that Westerners did indeed prefer a female body much more portly than my own.

I wanted, of course, to fit in, and I had no trouble adapting to my Arab hosts' taste in clothing, jewelry, or sandals. I soon did my best to have the right kind of gold necklace with red beads and the right kind of local dress, in light tie-dyed cotton for everyday and heavy indigo for special occasions.

Yet even as I learned intellectually to see in a certain fullness of figure the beauty they saw, I could not apply the same aesthetic to my own body. Should I try to get fat just while I was there, simply to fit in? The idea was impossible to, well, stomach.

I could pile my hair on top of my head as women did there, waltz about draped in desert finery, rub indigo on my lips, and put kohl around my eyes—even carefully veil my body and hair before older men. But to gain weight to comply with a foreign aesthetic felt like betraying myself and giving up my identity in a way that none of those other adaptations to local culture did. My own body ideal was just as much a construct as fatness was here, but it was too deeply integrated into my self-image to give up.

My difficulty in adapting to the thought that I should acquire a different kind of body is, I think, due to the fact that the bodily shapes and sizes that societies idealize are not so much fashion as they are physical manifestations of beliefs and practices that are anchored in a wider set of cultural values. For me, the sleek, streamlined female body I had been conditioned to emulate carried connotations of self-discipline, strength, industry, and general virtue. To change from wanting to look thinner to looking fatter was not like changing my taste in shoes, just because fashions changed. Much more was at stake: a whole set of values that I could not just shake off. I couldn't just shake them off because they were fundamental to the cultural world from which I came.

Where Do Body Ideals Come From?

Although there seems to be a tacit public assumption that Western society is marked by more extreme bodily ideals than ever before in history, and that those ideals are more hegemonic or oppressive than at any time in history, my own experience in Niger calls this idea into question. We are not unique in the lengths women go to achieve a bodily ideal, nor are we unique in how well developed the ideal is. To give just one example in addition to the desert Arabs I have described, the late Yale art historian Sylvia Boone studied girls' initiation among the Mende people of Sierra Leone in West Africa. She found that what women (and men) were most fascinated with were their own ideals of beauty, inculcated largely in initiation ceremonies. Boone had enough material to write an entire book about the highly detailed and developed ideals of body, face, and hair that people described to her, including high buttocks, a plump body, very dark and oiled skin, and graceful movement.[3]

According to Nancy Etcoff, a professor and psychologist who has researched beauty ideals historically and cross-culturally, ideals of body shape and size have probably been around as long as modern humans have.[4] There is a degree of arbitrariness to the ideals: neck rings here (Burma), nose rings there (India), a well-shaped male calf here (historically, in the West), a lotus-shaped female foot there (China). But body ideals are also grounded not only in cultural values but also in environmental realities and economic orders. Generally speaking, fat bodies are appreciated where food is hard to come by, and thin ones are admired in places where food is abundant. Since food abundance has been relatively rare historically, it is not surprising that, according to one estimate, around 80 percent of human societies on record have had a preference for plumper women.[5] Because humans evolved in environments of scarcity, they developed (unfortunately for us today) a desire for fatty foods and the ability to store fat easily—for women, in their behinds and stomachs.

In tandem with greater food security, but also with vast social and cultural changes, today modern Western ideals of slenderness seem to be sweeping across the world. Even in West Africa, where traditional beauty contests have long celebrated zaftig female bodies, things are changing. In the 2001 Miss World beauty contest, Nigeria, after performing poorly for years, entered a tall, svelte young woman whose skinny appearance appealed to few in Nigeria itself. She won. In the time since then, many women in the younger generation have quickly begun adapting to the Western-inspired ideal, especially in more urban areas, even as older Nigerians shake their heads in dismay. This revolution in national aesthetics is not taking place in a vacuum. The way has been paved not only by Western cultural influence but also by economic changes that make it possible to see the body in a new way and that make new kinds of bodies desirable.

But in a society like that of Nigerien Arabs, where a former slave population still does much of the cooking, water-carrying, and grain-pounding, an elite Arab woman's achievement of weighty immobility signals her ability not to work—indeed, makes it impossible for her to work. Their economy is also based on the herding of animals and long-distance trade, all carried on by men. When women drink the milk from men's animals and eat the grain men buy with their earnings from trade, they become potent symbols of their menfolk's success, transforming the goods men produce into desirability. Women's bodies thus constitute a convenient and symbolically potent place for men to invest their earnings.

A capitalist economic order like that of the West, on the other hand, needs both male and female bodies as workers and as consumers. Cultural critic Susan Bordo has pointed out that this means that individuals need to be self-disciplined and diligent workers, like the orderly and hardworking machines that have been the basis of our economy since industrialization.[6] Our bodies should reflect these values in the sleek, efficient, machinelike contemporary body ideal. But since capitalism encourages—indeed, requires—the never-ending expansion of markets and the purchase of the commodities that are produced for those markets, we are also exhorted to consume and indulge. By this logic, our bodies should be anything but self-denying and machinelike; instead, we should give in to our every whim and fancy. This tension between production and consumption, argues Bordo, creates the tension that pervades women's lives especially. Men are still the prototype of the productive worker, but women are now expected to both work outside the home and remain the primary shoppers and consumers. We should work out at the gym and restrain our appetites in order to express our diligent, energetic, and efficient natures as individuals (i.e., workers). But we should also indulge as dutiful consumers, in all manner of things available to us through the marketplace, not least the Big Mac, tall latte, and the jumbo muffin.

And yet, neither the environment nor economics determine bodily ideals entirely: otherwise, all people who live in deserts and herd animals for a living would have the same beauty ideals, which they don't.

Social orders and cultural values also play their part in making one type of body seem more pleasing than another. For Nigerien Arabs, for example, overarching notions of male and female make fat women and skinny men seem natural and desirable. Women and men are considered by Nigerien Arabs to be very different types of creatures, and their bodies should reflect this in fleshy, immobile femininity and hard, upright masculinity. A thin woman is considered "like a man" just as rounder men are considered slightly feminine. Women can actively abet the gender difference intended by God by making their bodies as different from men's as possible, i.e., by getting fat.

In the West, by contrast, where women and men are now thought to be essentially similar, women are expected to resemble men in ways bodily as well: hard muscles, able movement, none-too-exaggerated curves.

Another cultural factor that contributes to the fattened aesthetic in Niger has to do with conceptions of a healthy body. In stark contrast to the West's machine-model bodies, Nigerien Arabs see bodies more like the vessels they use for cooking and carrying water. They are potentially leaky, contain potent substances, able to be opened or closed, and—at their most healthy— they are full and cooking!

A healthy body should also, for them, be balanced in terms of the forces of "hot" and "cold" that are thought to pervade the universe. To be not too hot and not too cold means having a body that is quite "closed off" to the world around it, rather than "open" to all the winds and spirits that could enter it. Women are at an immediate disadvantage in achieving this healthy, strong, closed off bodily state, because, as the Nigerien Arabs say, women have three openings rather than two: a mouth, an anus, and a vagina. Women even sometimes playfully referred to themselves as "the cut ones" referring to their "open" genitals. When you are open, you get "cold," and women find themselves in the unfortunate position of being open all too often, notably when they have sex, when they menstruate, and when they give birth. Getting fat helps make one closed off and hot. It does so both by filling the body with energy, and by enclosing that energy by swelling the body and its openings.

If our body ideals are not entirely arbitrary but embedded in many aspects of our lives, then this explains, at least in part, why we are held so deeply in the thrall of how we think our bodies should look—in the West as in remote Niger. This, one may note, is at odds with the idea promoted by Naomi Wolf [7] and others that female body ideals are the result of the patriarchy, capitalist enterprises, and the media. Clearly male desire, media images, and advertising have a lot to do with why women go to great lengths to make their bodies look particular ways, why they feel intense pressure to do so, and why they may suffer greatly trying to meet the ideals. But it is a matter of anthropological record that many societies without capitalism or media images and with varying degrees of gender equality have preferences for how female bodies, in particular, should look: usually youthful, curvaceous, and plump. And women in many places expend considerable effort trying to live up to the ideal.

While it seems counterintuitive that those thin, willowy models staring down from billboards aren't somehow the engines behind the compulsion we women in the West have to look sleek and slim, my four years living in a culture without any media images whatsoever, but with a body ideal every bit as pronounced and sought after after as ours in the West, has convinced me otherwise. The pictures of trim and trained, airbrushed, collagen'd and Botox'd bodies could disappear from our visual world, and it is not likely, I now think, that we would cease striving to get our bodies to look a certain way.

Reading the Body: Fat Is Sexy

When I traveled to Niger, I was interested in "the body"—then a hot topic in the social sciences. With time, however, my interest in the body as a purely social symbol waned. Instead, I came to see the body more as my Arab hosts seemed to see it: as a potential object of beauty, and as an object of sexual allure. The fattening that these Arab women engaged in was certainly a kind of cultural work, expressing in physical form many cherished values and reflecting the social order. But to Nigerien Arabs themselves, the fat female body was largely a simple matter of aesthetics. Just like thin bodies in the West, fat bodies in Niger were appealing because they were, quite simply, attractive.

Even if biological realities, economic circumstances, gender constructions, and conceptions of health and the body underlie Nigerien Arabs' appreciation of fat women, it is not in these terms that they talk about fat women. In fact, they don't talk about fat women much at all, not only because of fears about the evil eye, but also because fat is ultimately about sex, and sex is something you don't talk about. When I spoke lightheartedly with teenage boys about the beauty of fat women, though, their insolent response was telling: they squeezed the air with their hands, in imitation of the pleasures of making love with a fat woman. When I gently broached the topic of the appeal of fatness with a woman known for her lack of appropriate reserve, she shot back, clearly annoyed at my naïveté, "Look, would you rather sleep on that mattress over there or on this hard ground?"

The sexiness of rolls of fat, stretch marks, and large behinds that girls invest so much in achieving here, however, creates a bit of a conundrum for women. For, as in so many societies, Nigerien Arab females should be sexy but not be too eager for sex. So how do you consume voraciously and sexualize your body while simultaneously distancing yourself from sexuality? Fattening and fatness itself, it turns out, contain plenty of room to do both: to excite *and* deny sexuality.

As girls flesh out their bodies, creating the contours of Rubenesque, fertile womanhood through their unceasing ladlefuls of porridge, they are expected to become ever more silent and still. Once breasts and pubic hair appear, women begin to veil their increasingly desirable bodies. And as they grow older and fatter, movement becomes more difficult, so their activity is curtailed, even as they excite lust in men. And, in a familiar logic, the more unattainable women are, the more they appeal.

In other words, while fatness is highly arousing, it also imposes an immobility and closed-off-ness on women that is thought to protect them from the potential dangers of sexual forces. Fatness is thus simultaneously a condition of desirability and a means of keeping female sexual lust in control—under a veil of fat, as it were.

Individualism and Body Ideals

Both Nigerien Arab and Western body ideals contain numerous "messages." Both are rather extreme; both are largely unquestioned in their respective societies; and in both places, women devote considerable time and energy to achieving them. Yet in the West today, the slender body ideal is experienced by many women as deeply oppressive, morally wrong, and a menace to young girls, even as women continue to emulate it. This is in stark contrast to the Nigerien Arabs. Women there did not seem to regard the imperative to be fat as problematic or troubling to their sense of self in any way.

This struck me as a paradox. Why did Western women, with more opportunities and more power than women have had at any time in history, feel so threatened by their beauty ideal, whereas Nigerien Arab women, with seemingly much less agency in their lives, do not seem threatened by their equally extreme body ideal? One could argue that precisely because Nigerien Arab women lead more circumscribed lives, the constraints on their bodies are not experienced so acutely. But the puzzle is this: in the West, where women choose their own partners (and can choose to divorce them), choose their own careers (and can actually have careers in the first place), and choose their own personal styles in clothing and adornment, why do so many feel so helpless and threatened in the face of beauty ideals? How do women with so many concrete freedoms and opportunities simultaneously feel victimized by an abstraction?

I believe the pressure women feel from body ideals in the West has little to do with the ideals themselves, as we tend to think. Instead, it has to do with the social context in which we try to live up to those ideals. Specifically, it is our culture of individualism and achievement that makes our bodily ideals feel so oppressive.

If a Nigerien Arab woman fails to get fat, this is thought to be due to her innate constitution, or because she is ill, or because someone has bewitched her. In the West, on the other hand, where we have the *freedom* to develop an individual identity, we also have the personal *duty* to do so. It is up to each individual to determine his or her own fate, and characteristics—from temperament to appearance—are readily interpreted not as givens but as under an individual's own control and design. Thus, if a woman fails to live up to the ideal, it is thought to be her own fault.

The opportunity to invent oneself imposes a great burden on the psyche as well as on the body. If we lived, by contrast, in, say, an African village where every individual's life course was far more predetermined, a woman in an advertisement might not automatically be read as a reproach or reminder of personal failing. Who a woman's father is, what village she lives in, what social group she belongs to—these are the things that define the parameters and possibilities of her life in this Nigerien society, not her own efforts and ambitions, although they, of course, may also affect her identity and the outcome of her life.

In the West, where we are not so tightly embedded in social networks that give us our identity, we have to search for ways to be and ways to look, and thus the available role models and images can have enormous pull. I suspect that if images of women representing various body and beauty ideals were to come to remote Niger, women might get inspiration for a new hairdo or jewelry from them, but they would not feel challenged, threatened, or taunted by the images the way many women in the West seem to feel. Their lives are not a self-designed project in the way the lives of women (and men) in the West are. The sense of inner responsibility for each pound lost or gained does not carry the weight, so to speak, that it does for women in the West.

The nature of eating disorders reflects this, for while most women in the West are exposed to images representing the coveted thin body ideal, it is girls at the ages when they are expected to develop their identities and define themselves as women who are most prone to develop anorexia or bulimia. And to the extent that eating disorders are beginning to crop up outside the West, it seems to be in societies and situations where women have gained increased freedoms and where an emphasis on achievement and individualism is beginning to be felt.

Free at Last?

Is it depressing or liberating to learn that women in the middle of the Sahara desert, without *Baywatch*, MTV, or *Seventeen* magazine, also devote much of their energies to achieving a particular body ideal? I hope that it is liberating to realize that our contemporary Western bodily ideals are just one of many possible sets of ideals. And it should be sobering to learn that our society does not have a monopoly on beauty ideals—even extreme ones.

Even after two years working at the health clinic in Niger, I still took off my sandals when I stepped onto the scale. I still felt a twinge of happiness if I weighed less rather than more, and I still thought my life was going better if I was thinner rather than fatter. But I also had come to see the beauty of those around me in their fatness. I, too, found a thin Nigerien woman less attractive than a fatter one, and when I came home to the United States, I began to find American women who approximated the Nigerien ideals attractive, even if I still held to the thin ideal simultaneously. (I have met a few women back home who would be considered absolutely luscious in Niger—but I refrain from telling them for fear that they would take it the wrong way.)

Then, after returning to Niger after my initial stint, and living in the desert with Nigerien Arabs for two years, I finally did start "reading" even Western slenderness in a new way. Thin women started to appear severe and manly to me, as if their bod-

Author and friend in Niger. Photo courtesy the author

ies were denying life rather than affirming it, pulling back from
sexuality rather than celebrating it.

Ironically, I have pondered the cultural pressures that make
women want to be thin so long that I no longer feel the pull to be
thin, even if I understand it intellectually. This change of mental
attitude has not led to any change in my weight; it just freed up
the part of my female brain that I have seen jokingly labeled in a
cartoon as "Things I Shouldn't Have Eaten."

Most of all, however, I have come to feel that body ideals, as
recurring aspects of human societies both historically and cross-
culturally, are part of important cultural work humans engage in.
Working to live up to a bodily ideal is to engage in making life
meaningful and bringing the pleasure of beauty into the world,
however one's particular society defines it. It is a shame that

it has become such an odious, even illness-inducing task for so many women in the West today. But, fat or thin, it may be difficult to eliminate the ideals themselves. Better, perhaps, to work on our own attitudes toward them, helped at least a little bit by knowing about places where fat itself is ideal.

Oil

Anne Meneley

I'm staying in a charming Tuscan villa that looks as if it has existed from time immemorial, on a lovely olive and wine estate.
Tuscany in mid-November is misty and cool, lit with a luminous
light. The view from my room: cypress-lined drives, rolling hills,
and picturesque terra-cotta farmhouses nestled amongst olive
trees. In the tiled dining room surrounded by charming examples of Italian pottery, we sip the famed Italian sparkling wine,
Prosecco, and graze on newly cured plump green olives. We taste
and compare five of the more expensive Tuscan extra-virgin olive

oils, each from a particular estate. We ask each other: a hint of watercress? A peppery aftertaste? We are newly minted olive oil connoisseurs, after all. We rave about our intriguing visit to the *frantoio*, the olive mill, where the air is moist and oleaginous and the people with their olives so photogenic. Exquisite courses follow, one after another, each coupled with a different wine . . .

I feel myself starting to wax rhapsodic, as if channeling one of the myriad food and travel articles about the unmitigated aesthetic and gustatory pleasures of Tuscany. The kind of writing that exudes the breathy impression that the only crises that one may face in Tuscany are those of food and wine is a style of which I am usually skeptical. Of course, I'm imitating it rather badly, since I can't really remember exactly what we ate that night, nor the names of the olive oils after the third (fourth?) round of prosecco. A real aficionado of this discourse, like *Under the Tuscan Sun* author Frances Mayes, would be able to describe the olive oil this way: "I think I taste the hot wind of summer in one, the first rain of autumn in another, then the history of the Roman road, sunlight on leaves."[1] One might finish with a lament that one won't *really* be able to properly reproduce the experience anyway, because everything tastes better in Tuscany. But I'm an anthropologist, not a foodie, and my interests lie elsewhere.

Why, I wondered, in this fat-phobic moment in North American history, is olive oil growing in popularity? Extra-virgin olive oil has become the sexiest and most desirable of the fat family of late. It has gone from "ethnic" oddity to household staple; it has displaced butter from the tables of fashionable North American restaurants. Butter, of course, has been demonized not only as a fat but also as an animal fat, bad for one's cholesterol. Even though the sudden reemergence of the Atkins diet equally demonizes carbs, trans fats—the solid, hydrogenated fats—are still making headlines. Fat has been dubbed "the new tobacco" and is the leading cause of cardiovascular illness.[2] Olive oil, in contrast, is at the center of the "heart-friendly" Mediterranean diet. As such, it is a "good" fat, a vitamin-rich, life-giving fat, as opposed to the fats that threaten life by hardening the arteries or disposing one toward diabetes. Yet, health concerns cannot be the only reason for the shift from animal fats, like butter, to olive oil: fatty fish oils are also promoted as heart-healthy, but it is hard to imagine dishes of salmon fat gracing the tables of chichi restaurants.

When I was sampling different extra-virgin olive oils at the tasting, I did not think about the fact that I was sipping straight fat—healthy or otherwise. Rather, I was trying to appreciate aesthetically the qualities of each oil. Extra-virgin olive oil is a fat that lends itself to being experienced and talked about in the language of discernment that many call "winespeak." The language of wine evaluation, whereby the taste and aroma of wines are described in reference to other tastes and smells, has inspired similar ways of evaluating not only olive oil but other luxury products like gourmet coffee, Scotch whiskey, and cheese. Like those products, extra-virgin olive oil requires knowledge and sophistication to be properly appreciated. Like good wine, it should be appreciated for quality over quantity; indeed, extra-virgin olive oil should be used not to fry but to adorn salads, vegetables, or bread. Extra-virgin olive oil is a good fat for contemporary North American palates these days because it is at once ascetic and hedonistic: ascetic in that it is healthy and consumed sparingly, and hedonistic in that it can be aesthetically appreciated as a tasteful luxury good.

But it is also a fat that is often associated with a place, as the term *Mediterranean diet*, of which it is a mainstay, implies. More specifically, it is a fat associated with Italy. Even though much of the oil that comes from Italy is produced elsewhere—in Spain, Greece, Tunisia, or Turkey—and merely blended and bottled in Italy, the impression that the producers strive to give is that the oil is Italian.[3] The reason for this is that Italian olive oil is described and marketed as being intertwined with Italy as a site of beauty and contentment. Discussions of the qualities of Italian olive oil will often begin with a statement like the following from Bausson and Chibois's gourmet guide to olive oil: "The colors and the perfumes [of Italy], the houses and objects, the cooking and the music—all come together in an ambiance very much resembling happiness."[4]

Not only things Italian, but particularly things Tuscan, are highly valued these days. Tuscany is not only noted for high quality olive oil, although Tuscan producers have been particularly successful in selling their extra-virgin olive oil on the international market. Tuscany itself is pervasively, imaginatively desired as a sensual place with a sexy cuisine. In foreigners' accounts of living or vacationing in Tuscany, we read endlessly of delicious meals in beautiful surroundings. Take for instance this snippet from Hungarian novelist Ferenc Mate's *The Hills of Tuscany: A New Life in an Old Land*, in which the author describes living in a Tuscan farmhouse with his wife, Candace. Here he recounts one of the most memorable gastronomic moments of his life:

> *Candace had asked for olive oil at the hamlet's store, and the owner took her down to his cantina where a big earthen jar was hiding in the cold, and ladled some thick oil into a jar for pre-*

*serves. So we spooned some of that over the sliced tomatoes . . .
and then we took a bite. And fell silent. We looked at each other.
What kind of flavors do these tomatoes have? They tasted peppery
and bittersweet, and tangy with a complexity that burst as it
passed over your tongue. Then we realized it wasn't the tomatoes
at all, but the opaque green olive oil that we'd poured over them.
We poured some more. We dipped bread in. We spooned it. We
dipped a carrot in it. We dipped our fingers in it. We licked the
forks. And we moaned like kids let loose in a pastry shop. It was
our first encounter with hill-grown, stone-pressed Tuscan olive oil.
One of God's great creations—now that we press our own, we use
a quart a week.[5]*

It is hard to imagine all this sensual dipping, licking, and
moaning about another fat, like margarine, for instance. And
extra-virgin olive oil is a fat that can be described as "one of
God's great creations." Even metaphorically, a fat like margarine
cannot be perceived as either divine or sensual.

Mayes's *Under the Tuscan Sun* seems similarly seductive for
readers, at least if its years on bestseller lists can be taken as an
indication. The book is a memoir of Mayes's relishing of the
sweet life—*la dolce vita*—in Tuscany, where she bought and reno-
vated a villa with her second husband, Ed, a poet. Many Italians
I met in Tuscany who had read the book said that it made life in
Tuscany sound not only sweet but perhaps a little too sweet. At
the same time, though, they said that *Under the Tuscan Sun* was
great for tourism, which keeps many Tuscans employed.

Of course, a book like *Under the Tuscan* Sun is aimed not at
Tuscans at all but at the non-Italians who wish to go to Tuscany.
It describes a life that does indeed sound sweet, with the chief

preoccupations being the acquisition and consumption of delicious food and wine. Mayes's house is beautiful, the air aromatic with flowers and herbs. Tuscan recipes adorn her accounts of shopping for the perfect seasonal vegetables or exquisitely produced cheese or sausages while visiting yet another picturesque hill town. Mayes and her husband themselves participate in this artisanal production, by picking and pressing their own olives, producing their own extra-virgin olive oil from their own trees. She writes:

> At home we pour a little into a bowl and dip in pieces of bread, as people all over Tuscany must be doing. Our oil! I've never tasted better. There's a hint of a watercress taste, faintly peppery but fresh as the stream watercress is pulled from. With this oil, I'll make every bruschetta known and some as yet unknown. Perhaps I'll even learn to eat my oranges with oil and salt as I've seen the priest do.[6]

The appeal of the book for legions of middle class North American readers is surely its tantalizing contrast to the lives that they lead at this moment in late capitalism, where people feel themselves to be under almost continual stress and the pressures of time. Time in Tuscany, if we are to believe *Under the Tuscan Sun*, moves at a different pace, more slowly, as if almost not of modern time. People take siestas in cooled tiled rooms, behind shuttered windows, something few employed North Americans can do. The book is structured seasonally, evoking a life ordered by an agricultural calendar instead of the needs of a corporate workweek. In North America, concerns about the safety of the food we consume often involve the anonymity of modern industrial food production. Foods can contain dangerous trans fats; it's nearly impossible to trace the meat in a hamburger infected with E. coli; distantly grown vegetables might be genetically modified to withstand packaging and shipping; foods may contain dangerous additives and pesticides. In North American grocery stores, we can buy produce from all over the world, in any season, but we don't know who the producers are or how they are producing it.

In contrast, Mayes describes buying meat from local people she knows, and vegetables that are grown locally, picked fresh, and sold in season. Or she grows her own—potatoes, for instance—to roast with her own rosemary and newly pressed olive oil. In the Tuscany that Frances Mayes describes, fast food, consumed alone and on the run, does not appear. Rather, meals are slowly prepared and consumed convivially. No dangerous fast food fats disguised with artificial flavoring appear here; food in Tuscany is drizzled with or dipped in healthy and naturally delicious fat, olive oil.

Following the Extra-Virgin

Consumers in North America and Northern Europe seem to view olive oil as an exception to a more general perception of fat as bad; indeed, in the aesthetic economy of fat, consuming extra-virgin olive oil is now a positive fat experience. I wanted to know how the Italian producers understood their country's beloved fat, now popular abroad. So I went to Tuscany to interview olive oil producers, who love to consume their own product, too, but their understandings of it, I learned, extend far beyond the delights of its consumption. Both producers and consumers value the same qualities of the oil, its full-bodied taste, and its virginity, but they do so in different ways. North Americans who comment on my research on olive oil invariably ask, "What's with the extra-virgin thing?"—bringing to the fore the link between oil and sex. Both producers and consumers seem to link olive oil to sensual pleasure. But I have found that producers of olive oil in Tuscany see the connections between sex and Tuscan olive oil differently than do its consumers abroad.

Technically, the term *extra-virgin* is now used to refer to oil that has less than 1 percent acidity. This grading is now established scientifically, but the way extra-virgin olive oil is talked about by producers and consumers suggests that its metaphoric power extends far beyond science. All of the olive oil producers that I spoke to displayed distaste for the "industrial" processing of olive oil. Each claimed a production style that at least evoked a traditional style of production—the use of a stone mill to grind the olives, for instance—as a way of claiming an authenticity for their oil. But what struck me most in conversations with Italian olive oil producers was their reference to the themes of purity and danger, their use of metaphors of religious and sexual notions of purity and pollution, metaphors of surveillance and enclosure, and concerns for establishing authenticity.

I was told of a Tuscan proverb that says "Your oil is more important than your wife." Another is "Oil is the mother, wine is the sin." Oil is referred to as if it were a virginal daughter who must be kept secluded from taint, but also as a chaste mother to be revered. Olive oil was the pure "lean" fat of Lent in medieval Italy; lard was thought to be an indulgence.[7] The complicated connections between the sexual and the sacred are also evident in the fact that when a bottle of extra-virgin oil is broken, one is supposed to call a priest to get the house exorcised. It is as if the virgin olive oil, escaping its vessel, spreading across boundaries, out of control, penetrating where it is not supposed to, requires a strong ritual hand to restore virtue.

This connection between sex and olive oil came up during a conversation with a family of former sharecroppers who operated a mill in the province of Arezzo, in Tuscany. I spoke with the patriarch and his middle-aged son, who was currently running the mill. In the midst of the son's explanation of how they retained the old stone mill to ensure an authentic cold-pressed oil, his father jumped up to interject, "These young people, they can't make love!" Here he made a screwing motion with his hand. "They eat the industrially processed oil without the vitamins and goodness of the virgin olive oil. Italian women are going to be very worried if men continue to eat mass-produced oil, because their men are not going to be strong enough to satisfy them sexually."

Of the mass-produced oils of which he spoke, the very worst kind is called sansa oil. The dregs of the olive pressing, the crushed pits and skins, are chemically treated until they become "fit, if not desirable for human consumption," as one of the increasingly ubiquitous olive oil guides describes it.[8] It is highly processed, brought to the accepted acidity level only through chemicals and steam. Sometimes this sansa oil has a little extra-virgin oil mixed in to add color, and according to my Italian informants this is often sold as "light" olive oil to North American consumers, who are fooled into thinking that the label means light in calories, which it is not.

As we were sitting drinking an espresso in the central square in Cortona, my young Italian tutor explained his theory that

North Americans are more flabby than sexy because they consume this sansa oil when they eat their daily buckets of french fries. I protested that not every North American ate french fries every day, but clearly I did not convince him, especially as droves of weighty North American tourists tromped past us, unabashed in their shorts, baggy T-shirts, and jogging shoes, in stark contrast to the slim and chicly adorned Italians. My tutor seemed to find this topic a good deal more fascinating than our Italian lessons: he relentlessly detailed his thoughts about the connection between the kind of fat consumed and both moral and physical qualities of the persons who consume them. Consuming mass-produced, cheap, commodity oil denuded of the healthful qualities and distinctive taste of the olive produces bodies that are swollen and unkempt, not capable of discerning good taste from bad, neither healthy nor attractive.

One Bad Olive?

This kind of industrial fat is the opposite of sexy; extra-virgin olive oil, in dramatic contrast, is a fat that is both sexy and virginal. Producers in Italy are vigilant about their virginal oil.[9] The taint imparted to bad oil cannot be expunged, as Lorenza De' Medici, the famous culinary author, olive oil producer, and cooking school diva, notes: "As anyone knows who has developed a taste for fine extra virgin oil, bad oil cannot be disguised by any amount of cooking or seasoning. It is immediately detectable and will ruin the taste of your sauce."[10] Thus, like parents following their daughters around on the *passeggiata*, the evening stroll through the town, to ensure that their reputations are not besmirched, owners of olives are vigilant and suspicious, following their own olives throughout the entire processing, even if they know and trust the miller. One olive producer, Maurizio, told me that you had to pay even *more* attention to your olives than to your daughter. Olive producers know that, as with sex, olive oil, once no longer virgin, can never regain its virtue. When I asked Maurizio the question that I've so often been asked, "What's with that extra-virgin thing?" he laughed and said that it is more about marketing than anything else. After all, he quipped, olive oil is like a woman, who can either be a virgin or not: how could either be extra-virgin?

Italian olive oil producers refer to extra-virgin olive oil as "liquid gold," an unusual nickname for a fat, but apt indeed from the perspective of the North American consumer who now pays forty or fifty dollars for a 500-ml bottle. Those Italian olive oil producers who receive an extra-virgin grade get a subsidy from the government to use toward the next year's oil. It also means they can sell their oil for more money. Yet olive oil producers are not solely concerned with financial gain. Those who bring their olives to the same mill are highly competitive with one another, and the purity of their olives and the resulting oil is a point of honor for them. The quality of the olives not only affects the acidity level of the oil—and subsequently its grading as extra-virgin or not—but also the quantity of the oil. Producers watch every drop of the precious greeny-gold fat as it pours out and cast suspicious glances over their shoulders. The men—this is predominantly a masculine space—eye one another's oil, trying to gauge how many liters each man is receiving for each hundred kilos of olives. There is fierce competition down to the last liter.

I visited a *frantoio* (olive mill) one autumn with Maurizio. Although I had previously visited olive mills in the summer, the charm of the mill is not evident until it is in operation, which happens in Tuscany from mid-November to mid-December. The air was redolent of olives. The normally immaculately dressed Italians wore scruffy clothes, their hands black from picking olives. Each container of picked olives was adorned with a scrap of paper noting the name of the owner, which seemed largely superfluous given the close watch that each owner kept over his olives. What struck me most were the both challenging and defensive looks on people's faces as we walked into the *frantoio*. Everyone I talked to expressed a fear of the "bad olive." The reason for this soon became clear.

Everyone's olives are processed in the same equipment; the olives are first crushed in a stone press. The olive paste is then spread onto circular mats (*fiscoli*) and squeezed until the oil comes through and the sediment is left on the mat. The owners of the olives want to ascertain that olives that preceded theirs are pure. Acidity level (which is increased by bad olives) will affect whether the oil can be officially graded as "extra-virgin," so someone else's bad olives can affect the virginal status of one's oil. The millers, too, have to be vigilant about this lest their mill get a "bad reputation" as a "tainted" mill.

The relationship between olive owner and miller should ideally be one of trust: trust that the miller won't accept impure olives, which could then taint the olive oil of all the customers. It is the responsibility of the miller to screen out the bad olives. Yet the customers who bring their olives to the mill rarely leave it up to him. In fact, as Maurizio told me, as soon as you walk into the mill, you should look at the other men standing there, to see what kind of people they are. It was not quite clear to me how one would identify by sight a person who would have the temerity to pass off bad olives as good olives, ruining everyone's oil in the process, but Maurizio implied that it was self-evident. He described how he would peer into others' olive crates, asking their owners *when* they had picked their olives. What he wanted to know, he told me, was whether their olives were bruised or moldy. I asked Maurizio if he might not possibly insult people by questioning their olives. He retorted with a contemptuous shrug, "If you insult them, you insult them. Who cares? You will save your own oil. And those behind you, waiting to press their olives, will thank you for keeping the bad olives out of the mill." The subtext was that it was more important to defend one's oil than to be polite to purveyors of skanky olives, who clearly do not deserve the ordinary tokens of civility.

With the widespread practice of selling foreign oil as Italian, producers were concerned to establish the origins of their own oil. Questioning an oil's origin was something I heard over and over again, with people worrying that the label did not represent the product. Some claimed that you could only trust estates that guaranteed the origin of the olives. Others said it was best to see the olive oil bottled straight from the terra-cotta pot. People talked about nationalities of olive oil—both favored and despised. These territorial concerns seemed to evoke just as powerfully concerns for paternity and legitimacy: the desire to know with certainty of whom this olive oil was the progeny.

Concerns for an oil's origin and purity are evident in the promotional material for the Laudemio group, a collective of Tuscan estates that produce extra-virgin olive oil. In its signature bottle, this oil sells for close to $40 U.S. for 500 ml. The prerequisite for membership in the Laudemio group is location within a specific region of central Tuscany. Geographical origin is not the only qualification, however; when I asked an Italian if former peasants in this region would be eligible to join Laudemio, he laughed and said, "No, only the nobility can join Laudemio." Laudemio markets its "noble oil" by highlighting the noble descent of its producers, as if the oil itself were the spawn of the noble lineage. Its expensive promotional book, *An Oil Called Laudemio,* includes photos of the Laudemio members on their stunning Tuscan estates, and recipes for Laudemio oil offered by famous foreigners and Italians. Movie producer Franco Zeffirelli, for instance, claims that the Laudemio group has taken steps to stop the "bastardization" in the purity of the olive lineage. He says, "All we can do is hope that [Laudemio's] creators manage to keep it in the enviable position which it currently occupies of being the purest of the pure."[11]

This concern to protect extra-virgin olive oil against taint extends to the ways in which it is stored. The oil is enclosed in cool interior rooms, far from prying eyes. One Italian aristocrat showed me into his olive oil storage room, a pristine cold room in the cellar. It was this room—housing the large and shapely terra-cotta pots in which the extra-virgin olive oil is stored—that he referred to as "his kingdom," not his grand house, even though it was formerly a Medici tower.

Although my friend Maurizio let us see his wine cellars, something his assistant said not many people would do, he did not volunteer to show us his olive oil storeroom. He told us that after the oil was pressed, it needed to rest in dark and quiet, undisturbed. One is not supposed to smoke or use heavy scents when entering a mill or oil storage room; these odors could penetrate, spoiling the oil. Like wine, olive oil should be evaluated by color, aroma, and taste (*colora, profuma,* and *sapore*); like a woman, olive oil should make a good impression, cut a fine figure, a *bella figura*. With a deft gesture, Maurizio mimed the shape of a woman's body, slim yet full-figured; his wicked grin and wink suggested her allure. Extra-virgin olive oil is a fat that should itself have a *bella figura*, and it is also a fat that can ensure a *bella figura* in people.

Tuscan olive oil producers often claim that "Tuscan olive oil is the best. That is well known and that is why it sells so well." Whether or not this assertion is strictly true is perhaps best for professional olive oil tasters to judge. But what is true is that as Tuscan olive oil flows into North American markets, North Americans flow into Tuscany. So, as the commodity moves toward the customers, the customers move toward the commodity. Extra-virgin olive oil is one element of a prestigious cuisine that evokes sophistication and *la dolce vita*. It is a fat that achieves what seems to be impossible now: being aesthetically pleasing and healthy, alluring and unsullied, hedonistic and ascetic. Although North American olive oil consumers might not put it in quite the same way as my Italian tutor, they seem to be, implicitly at least, making a similar association between bad, processed, and tainted fats that lead to a flaccid and unhealthy body, and a good, natural, and virginal fat which lead to a healthy and attractive body, a *bella figura*. And in extra-virgin olive oil's carefully pressed, virginal form, this is fat that can be imagined as liquid gold or a gift from God. It is a rare fat these days that can be envisioned as both precious and divine, both sexy and pure.

White

Mary Weismantel

At the center of the movie *Dirty Pretty Things* is a gruesome object: a human heart stuffed down the toilet in a London hotel room. Its discovery plunges Okwe, the protagonist, into a sordid secret world where undocumented immigrants sell their kidneys in exchange for fake passports. As a symbol, this waterlogged heart offers contrasting meanings. As the mutilated organ of an unknown victim, it represents suffering and physical vulnerability; as the plot element that forces Okwe out of his frozen emotional state, it is also the emblem of the capacity for love. But as the node of the circulatory system, the heart also suggests the eviscerated center of the international political economy—a system that operates more like a toilet bowl than a healthy body. Cities like London attract immigrants like Okwe with a vision of freedom and prosperity, but—lacking money or power—they find themselves mired in filth and trapped in vicious circles of exchange in which they must give far more than they originally intended. Before long, they risk being discarded like so much human waste.

Audiences in the United States or the United Kingdom may imagine that it is only in international capitals like London or New York that one finds such stories. But in fact anthropologists working in isolated rural areas hear rumors, jokes, and horror stories that revolve around images like the heart in the toilet bowl. Riveting tales about stolen organs have sprung up in every corner of the world, from Africa to Asia, Brazil, and Guatemala, carried by word of mouth and by the Internet. Organ theft is a fairly new idea, no older than the successful development of organ transplant operations, which have turned the bits and pieces of the human body into potentially valuable commodities. Some horror stories blend these new themes with older ideas. Like the dirty secret in the movie, these tales describe a new fear: that global capitalism's voracious, ever-expanding appetite for profits has turned the bodies of ordinary people into just another natural resource to be mined for whatever bits can be sold. But to express this notion, these storytellers turn to imagery that comes from ancient local traditions of the grotesque and the fantastic.

In the Andes Mountains of South America, a favorite scary story is about the *pishtaco*, a terrifying white stranger who attacks unsuspecting Indians with a knife, dragging them off to caves and hanging them upside down to carve up their bodies. But what he removes from his victims is not their kidneys or their hearts: it's their fat.

In a famous version of the tale recorded by Peruvian folklorist Juan Antonio Manya in 1969, the pishtaco

> *rides on horseback, wearing riding pants, elegant, dazzling, with a white cap on his head, and the horse similarly well-attired. . . . He blows a hypnotizing dust over his victim, who begins to tremble . . . and is drawn inescapably towards him. Arriving at his side, [the victim] falls on her knees and into a deep dream; immediately [the pishtaco] begins to work on her buttocks, injecting a needle connected to . . . the receptacle for the fat, which he extracts with great expertise. When he is finished . . . he slaps her, and she awakens without knowing what has happened to her, without noticeable marks on her body . . . but the damage is irredeemable, and within fifteen or twenty days she will die.*[1]

In more recent versions of the pishtaco legend, the horse has been replaced by Mercedes-Benzes and SUVs, and the handsome killer's costume may be a leather jacket and mirror sunglasses, or white medical scrubs. In the 1980s, when the feared U.S.-trained counterinsurgency special forces known as "Sinchis" terrorized the Peruvian countryside, rumors spread that these troops were in fact bands of pishtacos in uniform, with special permits from the government that allowed them to kill Indians at will, in order to harvest their fat. The latest trends involve video: since 2000, the pishtaco has been reported to wield a magical camera that can extract fat from the people it photographs.

It is astonishing to think that fat removal—an operation that is even more popular among prosperous South Americans than it is in the United States—could be so feared. For Westerners, bombarded daily with advertisements that promise "body sculpting" and new ways to "melt fat away," the pishtaco might seem too alien to make much sense. But just as *Dirty Pretty Things* offers middle-class London moviegoers an unfamiliar glimpse of their city as it looks to the black and Arab immigrants struggling to survive there, these Andean tales of stolen fat hold up a strange but revealing mirror in which we can see what it means to occupy the American position of superprivileged consumer in the world economy, from the point of view of those who look in at us from the outside, excluded by their nationality, their poverty, and their race.

Like the heart in the toilet bowl, the pishtaco is an image of a world economy gone horribly amok. The pishtaco sometimes has sex with his victims, robs them of their money, or uses parts of their bodies for his own nefarious purposes, but his primary motivation is not a vampire's lust or a cannibal's hunger. What he wants most of all is to make a profit; he extracts fat in order to sell it. In using his pale and dreadful image, Andean storytellers graphically represent the process of extracting commodities from poor, peripheral areas of the globe as an act of violence, one that is starkly racialized. The face and body of this ruthlessly predatory capitalist is a white one, and his victim's is not. In these rural areas and poor neighborhoods, where the population is predominantly of native Andean origins, people find it easy to imagine a white man as someone capable of committing the most gruesome crimes in order to make money.

In the imaginary world of the pishtaco—a world based on the collective experiences of native Andeans—a chance encounter with a white man begins as a story with two characters, both alive. But by the end, the white man is even richer than he was at the beginning, and the Native Andean doesn't even exist anymore, except as a discarded carcass. In the secret operations conducted by the pishtaco, he extracts what he wants and abandons the rest—although he is oddly meticulous about sewing up the apertures of the body when he has finished, thereby disguising his theft.

Wanting Fat

It's impossible to imagine these stories becoming popular in the United States, where we dream of the surgeon's knife as a release from unwanted fat. Surrounded by fatty foods, for us, it's the inescapable temptation to consume that can become an oppressive nightmare.

It's different when what you fear is hunger. In the places where people tell these tales, many people experience extreme poverty or are surrounded by the sight of it on a daily basis. In this context, fleshiness is a sign of life and health; like gay men in the early years of the AIDS epidemic, these are people who get upset and depressed when they catch sight of a neighbor who has suddenly become skeletally thin. In this bodily economy, it is not so unrealistic to imagine that really bad luck could come in the form of a loss of fat.

In Bolivia, Aymara Indians told anthropologist Andy Orta that fat translates to well-being and strength; if you lose your fat, illness follows. In the high, cold Ecuadorian parish of Zumbagua, where I have done fieldwork for many years, people see health as having plenty of fat, and illness as a frightening state in which the body's fat layers melt away inexplicably, leaving a person weak and exhausted, vulnerable to death. Fat is also beauty: a woman abandoned by her husband and his family, struggling to survive on a diet of barley and water, stretched out her arms to me. "Look at how thin my wrists are," she said. "They used to be round and beautiful."

Nevertheless, the theme of fat that runs through the pishtaco stories cannot be entirely explained away as a rational response to poverty. After all, in Africa today and in Europe in the past, peasants and poor people have imagined their creepy nocturnal killers drinking blood and eating babies, not stealing fat. The pishtaco's peculiar predilection for fat reflects a singular cultural tradition that gives fat a special significance.

In the Andes, fat is almost holy: in traditional religious ceremonies in highland Bolivia, sacrifices to the mountain gods and the earth mother were composed of the rendered fat and dried fetuses of llamas. And one of the greatest of the pre-Columbian deities was Viracocha, "Sea of Fat," an image of awesome power. Fat also has great power to do good: traditional healers prize various animal fats to dress wounds and to use as medicines.

But it is worth remembering that in Europe, too, not only fat but especially human body fat was long prized as a precious substance with unrivaled healing powers. Anthropologist Beth Conklin, tired of fielding hostile questions about the "cannibal" history of the Amazonian peoples she studies, responded by compiling a list of "cannibalistic" medicinal practices from European history, most of which involved the use of small quantities of rendered human fat.[2] Indeed, one origin for the pishtaco story lies in Spanish behavior on the battlefield, where the conquistadores horrified their Native American opponents by cutting fat from enemy corpses to dress the wounds of their own soldiers, a widely accepted medical practice in the Mediterranean at the time.

Fat, then, has not always been perceived as aesthetically repugnant and dangerous to health. Instead, it has been variously seen as creating beauty in both men and women; as a sign of good health and prosperity; and as a substance with medicinal and even spiritual powers. This rich and sometimes forgotten cultural history can help us to understand the story of the pishtaco, including some rather unexpected notions about race. For in this story the fat of Indians is not the same as the fat of whites.

White Fat and Indian Fat

Our prejudices against fat people in the U.S. are not without race and class undertones. The fact that African, Native American, and Latin cultural traditions valorize large bodies as beautiful—and that, in general, poor people of all colors are heavier and eat fattier diets than the well-to-do—allows an ugly stew of hatreds to come together in the abhorrence with which we regard fleshy bodies, especially if they are dark-skinned, ineptly groomed, or cheaply dressed. But we don't make the assumption found in pishtaco stories: that the fat of different races is actually different. Native Andeans believe that the pishtaco seeks out Indian victims because their fat is better and more valuable. The Indian "feeds himself strongly with *chuño* and *kañiwa*" [traditional highland foods], villagers told the folklorist Manya, while the fat of whites and mixed-race mestizos is "liquid and of poor quality." Similar ideas can be found long ago: according to testimony from colonial witchcraft trials, bewitching an Indian required making a doll out of llama fat mixed with cornmeal; if your intended victim was white, you needed a doll made of pig fat and wheat flour, the typical white diet in the Andes, then as today.

Similar ideas about foods, race, and fat still surface today. In my field site in Zumbagua, people insisted that Indians have strong bodies because of the Indian foods they eat. Nothing pleased them like my willingness to eat those foods with them. Ironically, from our fat-phobic point of view, when Indians wanted to describe how nutritious and satisfying their organically grown, locally produced grains and vegetables were, they told me that eating these foods was "like eating fat"—a scarce, delicious substance that they were able to eat only occasionally.

There many other ironies that can found in the pishtaco story: for instance, that the fat of Indians is strong and good precisely because it is produced by a lifestyle and diet that prevents much body fat from forming. But as far as the audience is concerned, the real kicker is the plotline, in which Indians are the only ones who know how to produce good fat that is worth money, but they can neither keep that fat nor profit from it. Indians in these tales have two kinds of bodies. One is a strong body, healthier than that of whites because it was raised on ancient, nutritious crops that make "strong, dense, dry" fat, unlike the liquid fat of "unpleasant consistency" possessed by whites.[3] But by the end of the story the Indian is left with a different kind of body: weakened and drained of its fat by an invisible, involuntary process that leaves behind only a useless shell destined for death.

There are plenty of other stories about how Indians who once were strong end up with weak, fatless bodies, even if they never meet up with a frightening white man with a secret machine. The

Aymara explained to anthropologist Orta that too much physical labor burns up one's fat, filling the body with steam and smoke. A more eloquent statement comes from Gregorio Condori Mamami, a Quechua migrant from the Peruvian countryside who worked as a porter in the open-air market. Old porters in the market, he says, are all used up, "without the strength even to haul their own bones" through the city. "We move through the streets and markets like the damned," he says, "our tattered clothes dragging behind us."[4] I've seen it happening in Zumbagua: the happy, healthy teenagers I met in the 1980s are thin and sick now, worn down by poverty, anxiety, bad medications, family crises, not enough food, and too much hard work.

For the Andean poor, then, the fear of losing one's body fat—and with it one's vitality and health—is real. But how completely does this sad tale of impoverishment explain the pishtaco? In actual life, Indian fat seems to ooze away slowly and inexorably through a hundred hard knocks that sap the strength and the will. In the story, however, it's not just that the Indian character can't seem to hold on to his fat; there's a really bad guy who steals it from him and sells it to someone else.

Stealing Fat

What the pishtaco does to his victims is clearly a violent crime. In the many different versions of the tale, he wields a veritable arsenal of weapons and tools. He tears open his victim's bodies with a machete, a knife, a revolver, a shotgun, a machine gun, a bayonet, even a "curved needle for severing the spinal cords of animals" or "a long pig-sticker with a sharpened blade."[5] These last two weapons hint at one aspect of his job: he is a kind of butcher who treats the body of a human being as though it were an animal carcass.

But at the same time, he is like a surgeon, making delicate incisions and sewing them up again, so that his victims awaken apparently intact, only to slowly die from the loss of fat. For this part of the operation, the pishtaco is said to import specialized equipment from the United States, Germany, or Japan. Since the tellers of these tales have not always seen such equipment, their descriptions often resemble the gadgets they have glimpsed in the hands of foreigners. Once I started writing about pishtacos, many researchers who have worked in the Andes contacted me with stories about how they had overheard Indians commenting that their tape recorders, cameras, or computers look "just like" equipment used by the pishtaco. These are unnerving statements to hear—especially when, as happened to Nathan Wachtel in the 1990s, the people talking had recently killed a suspected pishtaco.[6]

But there is a third step to the operation, the most important one: once he has extracted the fat, the murderer sells it. What the pishtaco does to an Indian body is a theft, not just a murder: one person's loss of life occurs so that another may gain—and gain not just an immediate pleasure or the release of emotion, but an actual substance that can be converted into hard cash.

An old country woman from Ayacucho, Peru, told a tale that reveals her understanding of the racialized economics that underlie the pishtaco's actions. She had never been to Lima, the nation's capital, but she knew of a restaurant there that serves "a very delicious soup" made from the bodies of babies stolen from her very own community. The flesh, she said, is nutritious and "high quality"—but the price was low, because the meat had been stolen from Indians.[7]

Her version is a bit unusual; most pishtacos have found far more creative uses for their product. In fact, in collecting pishtaco stories, folklorists have inadvertently recorded an entire economic and political history of the Andes, from colonial times to the present.

The earliest pishtacos were priests and monks who used the fat of Indians as holy oil, to grease their church bells, and to shine the lacquered faces of their holy statues. These ecclesiastical origins may help explain one of the weirdest pishtaco stories of all, the "Niño Ñakaq," or "Christ Child Pishtaco." This well-known statue, which looks like other blue-eyed, white-skinned images of the Christ Child found throughout Latin America, stands in a church in Ayacucho. It is said that the Christ Child leaves his pedestal every night to harvest fat like other pishtacos, and that if one looks closely enough as he stands immobile during the day, one can see the telltale grease spots staining the hem of his gown.

These stories about priests and saints are easier to understand if we remember that, during the colonial period, European religious orders were the equivalent of today's multinational corporations: expansive global enterprises that competed to set up extractive industries in every corner of the globe, and employed thousands of workers using highly coercive methods not far removed from slavery. An Ecuadorian researcher showed me copies of documents purchased by the Augustinians from the Spanish crown that were a kind of hunting license for human prey. They gave the bearer the right to capture a certain number of Indians from the warmer, lower altitudes and bring them by force up to the sparsely inhabited grasslands of Zumbagua, where they were to work as shepherds. By the eighteenth century, Zumbagua produced thousands of bales of wool annually as raw materials for bustling urban sweatshops run by the same religious order—and also staffed by Indians. No wonder listeners heard the voices of captured Indians in the sounds of the church bells and suspected that a predilection for thievery lurked behind their priests' sanctimonious demeanor, especially since the priests themselves eagerly spread rumors that members of other, rival orders actually *were* pishtacos.

In succeeding centuries, the pishtaco gained new wardrobes: as the hacienda system developed, he began to appear in the stories wearing the boots, leather jacket and chaps of a *hacendado*; in the twentieth century, when soldiers invaded rural areas searching for revolutionaries, pishtacos were said to wear a uniform. The twentieth century also saw industrial pishtacos: a gringo in a mechanic's overalls, who uses human grease to lubricate airplane engines; a pishtaco working for the North Americans, who bought Indian fat to keep the electricity running in a factory. The most pungent reference to the U.S. comes from Peruvian anthropologist Enrique Mayer, who was told that the famous moon landing of the 1960s was made possible only by using a fuel made from the tender flesh of Indian infants.[8]

The White Body

If Indian fat is strong and powerful, Indians are nonetheless people who don't have much of it. It is the white body that appears in pishtaco stories—and in Andean folklore more generally—as layered with fat. Andy Orta recalled how an Aymara man butchering a sheep held up a thick membrane of fat that covered the stomach and showed it to him. The patterns in the fat, the man said, were just like the patterns on the shawls worn by the "senoritas" in the city. This strange analogy refers to the dressing style of urbanized peasants in Bolivia, who drape layer upon layer of shawls and skirts on their bodies until they take on a mountainous shape, like a fat sheep covered in wool. But it also talks about the bodies under the clothing, which were once Indian but have become white as they've moved to the city and prospered by making an illegitimate profit from their country kin.

If urbanized peasants who have started to live and act like whites are described as draped in a layer of fat, whites themselves are even more associated with fatness. In Peru, *Viracocha*, "Sea of Fat," originally found in a Native American myth, became a polite term used to address white men and a generic term for them. This practice lasted from the colonial period throughout the twentieth century.

No one is whiter than the pishtaco, and in what storytellers say about his body, we see how whiteness, fat, and a more general sense of material abundance come together. The tellers call the pishtaco white, but they don't talk about his white skin; indeed, many pishtacos have black skins or even a "dreadful purple face." He may have blue or green eyes, but his most common physical trait is simply that he is big—tall, plump, or simply enormous—and hairy.

What makes the pishtaco visibly white is his softness and fleshiness—the signs of physical inactivity, an indoor life, and a rich and abundant diet. And according to the story this bigness, fatness, and whiteness come partly from all the things that body carries, wears, and uses. Story after story, old and new, examines the pishtaco's gadgets, creature comforts, and luxury goods in elaborate detail: his Mercedes-Benz, his boots, his jacket, his sunglasses, his cameras, and his electrical gear. And these things are also commodities: purchased from the same global marketplace that rips apart the bodies of Indians in order to make things that might then show up as something a tourist owns.

Foreign researchers in the Andes quickly become self-conscious about all their belongings, even though they may have thought they were "roughing it." Nathan Wachtel, in a book about his terrifying experiences as a suspected pishtaco, ruefully lists the things that were so little to him but so much to the local residents: "My possessions bespeak my wealth: the gas burner, the cans of Nescafé, the inexhaustible supplies of cigarettes, the candles, the sleeping bag . . ."[9]

I, too, had to confront this uncomfortable realization as I learned to see myself with Zumbaguan eyes. The most unsettling thing was that I lost the illusion of some sort of genuine, shared, universal human identity. Instead, I felt acutely my difference from the vast majority of humans alive today, people whose limited material conditions make them much more like the residents of Zumbagua than myself. I really did have a different kind of body, not because of genes or phenotype, but because of a long process of daily modification that had produced a physical self accustomed to certain kinds of possessions and products. What made our two races different, I felt then, was our daily exposure to two very different kinds of material worlds.

I realized all this because of the polite but nevertheless relentless scrutiny to which people in the parish subjected my body. They noticed everything, even the altered texture of my hair when I returned from trips to Quito, the capital city, where I applied conditioners in hotel bathrooms. Excruciatingly self-conscious under their gaze, I searched in vain for the boundary between my "real" self and the social history they read so accurately in the eyeglasses that helped me see, or the cushioned interiors of my hiking boots in a place where most people lack any shoes at all.

It's not so surprising, then, that one of the biggest markets the pishtaco has found for his product is as an ingredient in cosmetics, lotions, and luxury soaps: things that wealthy people use to alter their bodies, to make them softer and smoother—and things that really do contain high concentrations of fats. I was surprised to discover that some of the most appreciated gifts I could bring to Zumbagua were skin lotions and cold creams— things that, like other middle-class Americans, I took for granted. In the high altitudes of Zumbagua, the sun is strong and burns easily; the dust-laden winds and the smoky cook fires on which women prepare meals devastate their faces, lips, and hair. Women who had worked as domestics in the city reported back with awe and envy about the contents of wealthy women's medicine cabinets and dressing tables: the oils and creams that claim quasi-magical abilities to erase damage and reverse aging—and, in Latin America, are also said to whiten dark skin, straighten kinky hair, or curl the straight hair of an Indian. Pishtaco stories draw a direct line between the dry, cracked skin of the women I knew and the overstocked dressing tables of the wealthy: the fats that smooth and soften those wealthy skins are stolen from Indians.

As early as the 1950s, it was said that Indian fat was used to make skin lotions. Recently these sorts of cosmetic and pharmaceutical uses are heard of more and more, a trend perfectly appropriate for the current phase of late capitalism. Today the core nations of Europe, Japan, and the United States—together with elite enclaves throughout the world—are still the economic engines driving the world economy, but not as industrialists in need of labor and raw materials. Rather, it is as hyper-consumers that whites dominate, fueling world economic activity through the demand for new and luxurious personal possessions—and, increasingly, for new and more perfect bodies. How fitting, then, that the pishtaco should abandon his previous interest in farming and factories, and concentrate on the more lucrative trade in pharmaceuticals and biotechnology.

We are strangers to the Andes, but these pishtaco stories are, after all, a tale about us. My time in Zumbagua, which I thought was a time for me to investigate Andean culture, was also an education about myself. The final coup de grâce came when I began having extensive dental work done during my occasional trips to Quito. My young companion Andres, prompted by his giggling friends, asked eagerly whether my new crowns had been carved out of pig's teeth. Revolted by the thought, I replied with a vehement denial.

"So it's really true, then," he breathed, transfixed. "They came from a dead woman, didn't they?"

In this image of a gringa with the teeth of a dead woman glued to her jaw, I saw an inverted image—Marx's camera obscura—of the unacknowledged relationship between my own life as a consumer and the impoverished lives of the people I had come to study. The story of the pishtaco, too, offers a weirdly distorted but nonetheless revealing image of the global economy as seen from the perspective of the most impoverished rural peripheries. Here the production of commodities appears as an accelerating cycle of destruction: fuels and lubricants, cosmetics and skin creams, even transplanted organs and dental crowns—all products we purchase and depend on—are made out of the flesh of non-white workers from poor countries, rendered through processes that stole so much from those anonymous producers as to leave them weakened unto death. The killer's people—us—fatten themselves on the bodies of Indians, but our flesh, while abundant, remains as sickly and unsubstantial as ever: still white, and still hungry for the products of exotic bodies from far away.

It's only a horror story, after all, and one not intended for our ears; but the tale may be worth pondering a moment more. According to these stories, race is not really our immutable destiny; it's more like a bad habit we might yet learn to outgrow—but only if we choose to do so. In contrast to other stories about whites and Indians, which invite us to wallow in a vague and generalized guilt that cannot be connected to anything we've actually done, nor located in the present, pishtaco stories insist that oppressive race relations are daily reconstituted through dozens of individual and voluntary acts of consumption and exchange, without which race itself would cease to exist.

This advice—that if we really want to erase the specter of racism, suffering, and poverty that haunts us, we must begin by thinking about the effect we have on the world as consumers—flies directly in the face of our most cherished beliefs as members of a capitalist democracy. Americans are vociferous in defending their right not to know, or to care, about the people who make the products they buy: after all, it is by being stripped of its social history that an object can attain the glamorous, fetishistic appeal of the commodity. It is this cleanness and innocence that the pishtaco story tries to strip away, bringing to light a mythic hidden relationship between multiple but seemingly isolated and unrelated moments of acquisition, and the miserable poverty suffered by rural Latin Americans.

In these particular horror stories, the climax is not the scene of torture or lingering death: it is the moment of profit taking, when what had once been human becomes commodity. The details of the pishtaco's appearance foreshadow this outcome and so signal the race of the killer. In the telling of these tales, the pishtaco's white body is an object of fascination and disgust, because embedded in its possessions and its flesh is the record of what it has done to Indians in the past, and the threat of what it is going to do again. The challenge that the tale offers to us is to redefine the meaning of the white body, not through denying its history or its present constitution, but through changing the very processes of acquisition, commodification, and consumption through which it is created.

Phat

Joan Gross

Big Punisher, or Christopher Ríos, burst onto the rap scene in the late 1990s. With his rich voice and brilliant rhymes, his first album, *Capital Punishment*, went double platinum and was nominated for a Grammy. Proud of his Puerto Rican heritage, which he described as "the heart of an Indian, the strength of a Black man, and the pride of a Spaniard," Big Pun brought Latino rap into the limelight.[1]

At 698 pounds, he was also enormously fat when he died.

Christopher Ríos had not been a fat child. However, specialists might have recognized an early eating disorder. Frustrated and angry with his heroin-addicted mother and violent stepfather, he would punch holes in the wall and eat the pebbles from inside. The term for this kind of persistent eating of nonnutritive substances is Pica, and it is often associated with nutritional deficiencies, parental neglect, and abuse. Ríos's stepfather used to wake him up in the middle of the night to do push-ups, and later his mother kicked him out of the house at age fifteen for refusing to continue selling drugs. Homeless, he slept at other people's houses, eating where he could. His hosts commented on his big appetite. When he turned eighteen, he suddenly found himself with half a million dollars, from a lawsuit filed for him after a childhood accident.

With money in his pocket, Ríos set about trying to satiate his appetite, and from this point on, his body size began to expand. Big Pun was respected in the hip-hop community as a good husband and father. He was considered "good" at these social roles because his wife had plenty of cash in her pocket and his kids had toys that other kids could only dream about. The wealth that made him fat also turned him into a "provider," and as such he was respected in his community. He was known as a family man and enjoyed interacting with his three kids. One of his interactions involved getting them to box one another. He would even wake them up in the middle of the night to fight. It was reminiscent of his own rude nighttime awakenings by his stepfather to do push-ups.

Big Pun made up for the lack of control exemplified by his ever-expanding body by exerting control over his wife and children. He wouldn't allow his wife, Liza, to have girlfriends, get an education, or even watch talk shows. In a show of dominance, he always insisted on eating her last bite of food as well as his own.[2]

She always needed to be there for him, and as he got fatter and fatter, she became indispensable. She bought him top-of-the-line, XXXXXX-Large T-shirts. Even these she had to stretch out, wrapping them around her body and tugging on the material, first in one direction, then in another, in order for him to be able to wear them. As he continued to grow, she continued to dress him. Soon all his clothes had to be custom-made. The immobility brought on by his fatness made Big Pun unhappier with himself and more abusive toward his wife, especially as he grew dependent on her to perform the most basic hygienic tasks. While his immobility increased his abuse of her, it also saved her. She could escape his brutality by climbing the stairs where he couldn't reach her. Once, knowing that from where he was planted in the dining room he couldn't see her packing suitcases in the next room, she tried to leave the house.[3] For twelve years Liza was a battered wife, the real-life manifestation of her husband's lyrics "Be larger than life, my initials carved in my wife. / She said she'd starve on a diet instead I'm a God in her eyes."[4]

People who were close to Big Pun worried about his weight, but he was the center of money and power in his family and neighborhood. No one could tell him what to do. His grandmother actually moved into his house to cook healthy food for him, but said that once she went to bed, he would order buckets of Kentucky Fried Chicken and hamburgers. His good friend Fat Joe, no Slim Shady himself, tried to help Pun diet, but people snuck Big Pun food because it made him happy.[5] Joe talked Pun into going to a fat farm. Pun lost eighty pounds but left prematurely and proceeded to gain an additional three hundred.

Pun didn't yo-yo as much as many obese people because he didn't think it was "cool" to be so controlled about his eating. He worked hard at creating an image of a man who was supremely in control and at the same time totally excessive and immoderate. It is no surprise that he would reject the sad and defeatist auto-biographies of overeaters.[6] Soon, however, it became even more uncool to be immobilized by his own weight, and he stopped making public appearances. Even when his tour bus stopped at a restaurant, Pun stayed in the bus and had others bring food to him. When his sister tried to get him to go to Disneyland, he answered, "Oh, yeah, Pun in a motorized wheelchair, how cool is that?"[7]

At the age of twenty-eight, Big Pun died of a heart attack. Fat Joe commented, "I'm used to young people dying by getting shot . . . I never seen a young nigga die because he was fat."[8]

Fat/Phat

Fat seeped into hip-hop culture through the music industry, where *fat sound* referred to heavily processed audio featuring lots of reverb, chorusing, or doubling. Unlike the use of reversal in African American vernacular English, whereby *bad* took on the meaning of its opposite, *good*, *fat* had positive connotations from the start, and was metaphorically extended to refer to a full, rich sound. This adjective expanded to other domains as a compliment paid to something or someone who is attractive. The identical sound of *fat* and *phat*, then, was not the result of sound convergence where two words from semantically divergent realms merged over time into homonyms. Instead, it was a case where the meaning of a single word was enlarged within American hip-hop culture and later differentiated by being spelled differently. Two different letters that represent the same sound replaced the single letter *f*. The desire to separate *phat* from the maligned state of *fat* in mainstream society points to the cultural ambivalence concerning fatness in the United States. This new spelling complicated the word and lent it a slight aura of prestige—the same process is at work when secondhand shop owners spell *junk* as *junque* or *old* as *olde*.

It seems that people further differentiated *phat* from *fat* as they reinvented its origin, saying it started as an acronym. "*Pretty Hot And Tempting*" is the most widely reported source, but other acronyms referring more specifically to parts of the female anatomy are cited as well in online rap dictionaries.[9] These run from the neutral, "*PHysically ATtractive*" to indexes of the fattest parts of female anatomy, "*Plenty o' Hips And Thighs*" and "*Pussy, Hips, And Tits*." But the adjective is not used exclusively to describe women: cars, songs and clothes are also frequently described as "phat," which gives the lie to its status as an acronym.

While "phat" is commonly used to describe attractive women, the actual fatness of rappers such as Heavy D, Biggie Smalls, the Boo-Yaa T.R.I.B.E., Fat Joe, and Big Pun lend the original word more of a male connotation. In an era that idolizes young emaciated women, these hip-hoppers lyrically redefine fatness as hyper-maleness. First and foremost in this definition of masculinity is control—being in control of other men, women, and financial resources. Through brute force, which is closely correlated with body size, men gain respect and access to wealth. Literally and figuratively they can throw their weight around. Fatness is not viewed as a sign of lack of control but as a means by which control is attained.

The definition and value of fat itself is a contested arena. The multicultural background of the United States brings with it alternate visions of what constitutes fatness, as well as the desirability of fat on bodies. One definition of the adjective *fat* in *Webster's Unabridged Dictionary* is split into (a) "fleshy; plump" and (b) "too plump; obese." There are worlds of cultural difference between "plump" and "too plump." Among African Americans, the obsession with thinness has never been as prevalent as in mainstream white culture. In *Fat Talk: What Girls and Their Parents Say about Dieting*, anthropologist Mimi Nichter reports that African American girls expressed a greater acceptance of their bodies than did white girls. They recognized that African American boys liked girls who were "thick" with "nice thighs."[10] Evidence of this can be found in lyrics from rap songs such as Sir Mix-A-Lot's "Baby Got Back" where he raps, "I'm tired of magazines sayin' flat butts are the thing" and "I like big butts."[11]

But African American girls cannot ignore the magazines and the dominant white ideal of beauty with its focus on thinness. For that matter, cultural critic Susan Bordo points to the increasing number of articles on weight, dieting, and exercise in African American magazines.[12] A review of the film *Real Women Have Curves* in the hip-hop magazine *Vibe* begins, "To hear Hollywood tell it, the world is full of people who are as skinny as they are blond." Here we see thinness acquiring a racial specificity—as white. Of course, Hollywood thinness does not represent the average white woman, either. There are plenty of fat blond Americans, but Americans of color have a much higher rate of obesity, with African American and Latino adolescents nearly twice as likely to be overweight than non-Latino white teenagers.[13]

Rich Fat, Poor Fat

Fat people have had increasingly difficult lives after World War II, as obesity has come to be seen as a sign of overconsumption and lack of self-control. Fat people are accused of eating more than their share. Yet, in the United States there is an ambivalence surrounding the consumption of all goods, including food. Shopping is defined as happiness, and consumption has even been designated a patriotic activity during the George W. Bush administration. Food is often part of shopping trips, and with supersize deals in fast-food chains, Americans are encouraged to eat more than they normally might.

On the other hand, those who can best afford to overconsume are careful not to do so in the realm of food, since eating too much leads to a body type that is generally not admired or envied. Richness and thinness are linked, as evidenced by the Duchess of Windsor's oft-repeated saying, "You can never be too rich or too thin." At the same time the meaning of *rich* overlaps with *fat*. As well as meaning "wealthy," *rich* is used to designate luscious food with a high fat content. Likewise, one can live off "the fat of the land," have a "fat wallet," or a "fat job," or simply be a "fat cat." To put it succinctly, *fat* means "wealthy," even though the wealthy stay thin.

Just as richness and thinness are linked, so are poverty and obesity. If obesity is more prevalent among Americans of color, it is also more prevalent among poor people of all shades.[4] The highest rates of obesity occur among people with the highest poverty rates: these are people who experience "food insecurity," defined by the U.S. Department of Agriculture as "limited or uncertain availability of nutritionally acceptable or safe foods."[5]

Rather than speaking of obesity as a disease of the already poor, cultural commentator Laura Kipnis calls fat a predictor of downward mobility. A fat person has a lesser chance of being hired or, if employed, of being promoted. Kipnis notes the anxiousness and ambivalence provoked by living in a society that deeply wishes us to overconsume, yet savagely punishes all bodily evidence of overconsumption.[16] Why, she wonders, is fat so ridiculed when other spectacles of overconsumption, such as gigantic houses and gas-guzzling cars, get layouts in magazines?

It could be that the hatred of fat encourages people to spend even more money, only this time on the multibillion-dollar diet and fitness industry that gets "fat" from the yo-yoing weights of millions of Americans. (A sort of fossil record of this can be seen in the various magazine covers featuring Oprah Winfrey over the years.)

Phat Style

Fat, then, is a common American trait more prevalent among people of color and poor people. These two categories overlap to a great extent, and they form the very culture that gave birth to hip-hop. The subculture of hip-hoppers adheres to a very different aesthetic. Many famous rappers who lead hip-hop style are overweight, and even obese. They often proudly proclaim their size in the names they adopt: Notorious B.I.G., Heavy D, Fat Joe, Large Professor, the Fat Boys, Pudgee Tha Phat Bastard, and Big Pun. They refer to themselves in songs as "overweight lover," "Big Daddy," "heavyweight Bronx champ," and even "big belly babalu boogaloo big boy." Also significant are comparative references to Buddha (the most overweight major religious figure) and sumo wrestlers. Largeness is equated with largesse in album and song titles like *Livin' Large*, *Big Tyme*, "Mr. Big Stuff," and *Big Poppa*. Then there's the FatBeats record company, a hip-hop magazine called *XXL*, and the hip-hop fashion houses Phat Farm and Baby Phat.

Very different aesthetics also exist for men and women. A spin through hip-hop fashion catalogs shows men's clothes sprawled out on the page, while women's are tucked in severely at the waist. Bill Cosby's beloved character Fat Albert appears on male sweatshirts, while a lithe cat is ubiquitous on women's logos. Male hip-hoppers go in for baggy clothes that generally hide body shape. Young men who are "ripped" (i.e., well muscled) appear bare-chested on occasion. But the more common garb consists of layers of baggy shirts (often jerseys) and pants hanging off the waist and piling up in ripples at the shoe. Rather than containing the body, these clothes appear to expand it. Even hip-hoppers of average weight cut an obese outline, and it is not unusual to see the puffed-up shape of rappers wearing bulky down jackets on album covers. From a European point of view, American style has always tended to favor looser clothes, but hip-hop style takes loose American clothes to an extreme, or, as one song puts it, "baggy as hell, double XL."[17]

While young women in hip-hop culture sometimes wear baggy pants and sweatshirts, they more commonly wear supertight clothes and bare their midriffs. Male rappers may rhyme about their preference for curvaceous women, but the women that you see hanging on their arms are considerably thinner than they are. Women's clothes contain them, so they take up less space, while men's clothing expands their bodies' contours so that they take up as much space as possible.

The reduction in the ideal size for women is occurring at the same time that women are beginning to gain power in other realms. This leads one to wonder, with feminist critic Naomi Wolf, whether the cultural fixation on female thinness is not about beauty but female obedience.[18] Female rappers who are overweight tend to be the most disobedient to gender norms. After her recent shedding of pounds (which she insists was purely for health purposes), Missy Elliott stated, "I have always been a big girl myself and I always took pride in the fact that I never had to change my body to be considered beautiful or successful."[19] When speaking about her 1999 album, *She's a Bitch*, Elliott explained that she was a bitch in power. "[S]ometimes we gotta be a bitch to get to a certain point. This is a male dominated field and sometimes if you're not that bitch, you know, people will take advantage of you."[20] Both Queen Latifa, a large woman, and Missy Elliott pride themselves on their intelligence, strength, and creativity. They don't deny their sexuality, but they do not play the familiar role of sex symbol, as do many of the thinner female rap artists like Foxy Brown and Lil' Kim.

Consuming Power

Fat activists work hard at getting the message out that people should not automatically think of gluttony and overconsumption when they see an obese person. They argue that fatness is unfairly persecuted as the result of a behavioral deviation, ignoring its genetic, environmental, and cultural aspects. Within the world of rappers, however (in particular, gangsta rappers), overconsumption is the name of the game. Gangsta rappers are obsessed with being rich as well as eating rich. Their lyrics describe having lots of money and spending it on diamond-encrusted jewelry and luxury cars. A brief inventory of lyrics contains Beemer, Lexus Coupe, Benz, Hummer, and Lamborghini. On "Glamour Life" Cuban Link raps with my "golden silk pajamas on, smoking havanas, drinking Dom P, counting my G's, I'm out to be a millionaire . . . I'm in to be the King of New York. Went from living in tenements to up in house resorts . . . sitting on top of the world like a sun." Inspired by Minister Louis Farrakhan, Fat Joe created a politically charged song in which he addresses economic self-determination: "now I understand the bigger picture / fuck crying about the struggle / I teach ya how to get richer."[21]

In addition to consumer goods, wealth brings women. As Big Pun said, "They used to say I'm too chubby / But since the money the honies got nuttin' but love for me.[22] In "What's Love," Fat Joe raps, "I'm a provider. / You should see the jewelry on my women."[23] Women rappers say that they don't want "players" and that they don't judge potential partners by what they can provide, but this view is not shared across the genders. A woman's ability and willingness to consume luxury items is considered an aphrodisiac of sorts in male gangsta rap.

Money is power, but in the aesthetic of fat rappers, body size is also equated with power, both as strength and as sexual prowess. Penis size is a common way that men measure their sexual ability. Media scholar Jerry Mosher writes of fat men who become alienated from their bodies as their penises are reduced in proportion to their body size or are rendered invisible by their protruding bellies.[24] But fat rappers declare that their penises grow in proportion to their bodies. Notorious B.I.G. raps, "I got more mack than Craig and in the bed believe me sweety I got enough to feed the needy." Big Pun devotes an entire song, "My Dick," to his penis, and in "Still Not a Player" he brags, "you couldn't measure my dick with six rulers." At the end of his life, his penis would indeed have had to have been extra long for him to be able to see it beyond his 698 pounds of flesh. In his hit song "I'm Not a Player" (which is all about being a player), the woman is told to do all the physical labor of the sex act.[25] This is framed as if the man is in control and tells the woman what to do, but it could also be read as a sign of helplessness in the context of Big Pun's increasing immobility.

There was a time when European aristocrats chose weightiness as a sign of capacity to rule. The same holds true in Polynesian societies, for example, where chiefs and their wives were typically heavier than commoners. Rappers appear to adhere to this same aesthetic, growing large and referring to themselves as "king" of their city. When Pun playfully challenged a friend in a stretch limousine where he took up the entire backseat, the friend said that it wouldn't be a fair fight since Pun was ten men.[26] Pun's *Capital Punishment* CD shows several touched up photographs of a bigger-than-life Pun towering over several New York landmarks. A mural in his honor, painted on a Bronx wall after his death, displays his huge body looming over the New York City night skyline: a figure who certainly cannot be overlooked. After his death his sister said, "I looked at my brother as strength, nothing could take him down."[27]

Strength and ample food and drink are often associated in rap songs. Luxury items like Moët & Chandon and Dom Pérignon champagne, Hennessey cognac and T-bone steaks, help create the image of high-roller partiers. In *My World*, Big Pun refuses to drink out of plastic cups. He wants "platinum plus crystal glasses with the fancy cuts," but in the two CD photographs of him eating, we see no evidence of crystal goblets. The inside photo of

Yeeeah Baby reminds one of the Last Supper, only with Chinese takeout. While his "dogs" seem to be discussing important matters, Big Pun looks beatific as he concentrates on his fast-food container. Lower-class or cheap foods are also commonly referenced in songs. A brief survey of rap lyrics brings up cheese eggs, fried rice, rib tips, Cheez Doodles, Chips Ahoy! cookies, grape soda, and Skittles.

Big Pun talks about "eating well and getting fat," and so he did, though in addition to the most transparent understandings, cooking and eating are metaphorically linked to both sex and violence in gangster rap lyrics.[28] On one hand we hear, "She got a body make a nigga wanna eat that," a lyric that highlights sexual appetite.[29] On the other hand, we hear about devouring enemies. Both Notorious B.I.G. and Big Pun referred to themselves as cannibals in different songs. B.I.G., after comparing himself to Jeffrey Dahmer, said, "I cook you up so quick they call me Biggie Smalls the Chef."[30] Big Pun rapped, "Cannibalism is livin in my metabolism . . . That's all my thugs thinking bout, drinkin your blood."[31] In other songs he warned, "the recipe is death and I'm the chef, fricasseein your flesh."[32] Here the act of eating or drinking is a violent act meant to control one's enemies—which may well include one's sexual partners.

Eating the American Dream

Historian Hillel Schwartz calls hunger a biological need motivated from within by the body's lack of what it requires. Appetite, on the other hand, is a desire.[33] In rap songs and biographies of rappers, hunger is evident in descriptions of the lives of poor people in urban ghettos, but the focus is on appetite and living the glamour life. Like the medieval French novelist Rabelais's gigantic character Gargantua, who revels in his gluttony, rappers embrace "unapologetic fat" that represents a lusty love of living life to its fullest.[34] Unapologetic fat attempts to mask the effects of hunger that are created by the lack of a nurturing environment and, often, a lack of food itself. Lack reminds one of one's defenselessness, one's small place in a world brimming with desirable yet unattainable objects. Fatness symbolizes the desire to take up space and be recognized.

The escape of hip-hop heroes from urban poverty to the acquisition of wealth and fame adheres to the beloved American narrative of moving up the social hierarchy through individual effort. But the stories diverge from the typical American success story in that in the rap narratives, social mobility is achieved through violent, illegal means—drug dealing and robbery—not legitimate work. (The actual intellectual work that goes into rhyming and marketing those rhymes is hidden from the listener.) On the other hand, the focus on consumer goods in the lyrics and lives of rappers follows the common American pattern that urges us to buy more and eat more. In this sense, while it does protest many aspects of mainstream culture, hip-hop culture does not escape the webs of American consumer society.

In the end, though, hip-hop does offer a different perspective on fat. For Big Pun and other fat rappers like him, fat bodies and phat music translate into fame and financial success. The celebration of corpulence in rap music contests mainstream American ideals and messages that tell us that fat is sad, repellent, and shameful. Rather than being a source of shame, in hip-hop, fatness is celebrated as a positive sign of power and attraction.

Porn

Don Kulick

One recent, lonesome night at the seedy Chelsea Star motel, my childhood friend Eli decided to price out some escort services with numbers culled from the back of a certain well-known NYC weekly. Realizing that his dream night was only to be a night of dreams, he headed out into the humid darkness in search of a less expensive way of sating his appetite. He came back with a cheese steak and one copy of Big Butts. *I had never known Eli—the person with whom, in the seventh grade, I viewed my first porn—to have a taste for larger women . . . But he does. And so, I imagine, do some of you.*

That little quote is the beginning of a review on fat hard-core films, in *The Village Voice*'s biweekly porn column, written by someone who calls himself Johnny Maldoro.[1] The review rates videos like *Chunky Cheerleaders: Obesity U*, *Chunky Chicks 19*, and *Scale Bustin' Bimbos 5*. It makes a lot of lame fat jokes along the way, and it concludes on the same note, with the self-satisfied chuckle that "sweet dreams are made of this."

The videos that Johnny Maldoro reviews are ones in which the women featured, for the most part, have some form of vaginal sex. The sex might be somewhat out of the ordinary: in *Chunky Cheerleaders: Obesity U*, for example, two women insert a long, fleshy dildo into each another's privates, but the camera focuses on how they then simultaneously eat out the centers of a couple of Twinkies. So it isn't exactly traditional hard-core porn. Nevertheless, some form of genital contact is depicted.

Beyond this kind of pornography—which differs from more conventional varieties only in that it features fat women—there is another kind of fat pornography directed at a more specialized audience. This is a pornography that many of us have encountered, usually without even being aware of it—often, it turns out, in shopping malls. It is displayed on the racks of greeting-card stores, in the sections reserved for gay birthday cards, fart cards, and cards featuring toothless old women. Interspersed in sections like this, you will often find a range of fat-lady cards. These will always depict full body shots of astonishingly obese woman, either nude or in see-through lingerie, smiling seductively and blowing kisses above captions like "It's Your Birthday, Let It All Hang Out" or "The Best Things Come in Big Packages." Next time you see a card like this, take a moment to consider that many of the models in those cards are famous in the world of fat pornography, where they are regarded as goddesses.

This kind of pornography specializes in women who weigh well over three hundred pounds. Some of the biggest stars tip the scales at more than five hundred pounds. Aside from the sheer size of these models, the single most striking thing about this genre of pornography is that the women who are pictured do not engage in sex. Instead, they pose: dressed in lingerie in their bedrooms, clad in bikinis or everyday clothes on their living-room sofas, standing naked in their kitchens. While they do sometimes display their breasts and their behinds, most of the camera work is focused on their stomachs. Genitals are generally not exposed, perhaps because once a woman passes the four-hundred-pound mark, it's frankly impossible to actually see her genitals without the aid of special equipment.

Instead of having sex, these women have food. They eat. Photos show them tucking into a pizza, spooning into a carton of ice

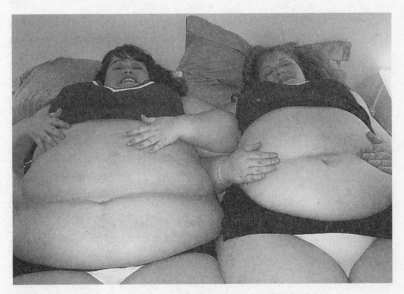

Reproduced with the permission of Heather Boyle of BIGCUTIES.COM

Reproduced with the permission of Heather Boyle of
BIGCUTIES.COM

cream, slurping spaghetti, luxuriating in whipped cream, pour-
ing syrup on a stack of pancakes, biting into a bun.[2]

The pornographic act is not the display of a penis or some
other object entering a woman's vagina. Instead, the pornographic act is the display of fat food entering a fat woman's
mouth. Look at the racy promises made on a Web site advertising
videos for this particular erotic market:

> *"Sandie—The Boudoir Video" is a private peek into a fat woman's*
> *boudoir and bath . . . This video features Sandie in revealing*
> *lingerie, moving and dancing and smiling seductively. There is an*
> *extremely provocative eating scene, not to mention her playful ex-*

perience with a large bowl of whipped cream, for those of you who enjoy eating fantasies. And finally, we see all of Sandie in her 350 lb nude exuberance, enjoying herself in a heart-shaped Jacuzzi tub full of bubbles. (Tasteful nudity) 55 minutes, set to music.[3]

"Tasteful nudity," indeed: the playful experience with the large bowl of whipped cream electrifies that phrase, opening it up to a whole new range of possibilities and meanings.

Here's another teaser, this one from fat porn diva Supersize Betsy's Web site:

My new video includes: my eating a huge breakfast-in-bed in the nude . . . me walking in the nude . . . me being tied down and fed two quarts of cream through a thick tube (thicker than previous video—so it flows into me very fast! My belly also "sits" on the bed beautifully in this scene) . . .[4]

What, one might ask, is going on here? Are scenes of eating like this really pornographic? Yes, they are, say fans. The first issue of the now-defunct lesbian zine *FaT GiRL* ("A Zine for Fat Dykes and the Women who Want Them") contained no less than eighteen photos of hefty women, most of them fully clothed, feeding each other grapes, whipped cream, ice cream, and other foods.[5] Issue number two published this letter from a reader:

I think my favorite part of the first issue . . . were the photos of the women feeding each other. So pornographic!!! I don't think I've ever seen pictures of big women eating, happily eating, much less feeding each other with such obvious enjoyment. Those pictures just shot an electric current through me.[6]

Others who clearly find such pictures erotic are individuals who identify as "feeders" and "feedees." A feeder is a person who gets pleasure out of encouraging and helping another person gain weight. A feedee is someone who enjoys gaining weight, especially when assisted by a feeder, in the context of a sensual or a sexual relationship. The ultimate sign of commitment in a feeder-feedee relationship is when the feedee allows herself to be "taken to immobility" by her feeder—that is, when she is made to gain so much weight that she is unable to walk. Women like Supersize Betsy, who is one of the best-known feedees, speak about this in romantic terms. At over five hundred pounds, Betsy told an interviewer that she thought she could only put on about another eighty pounds before she reached immobility. But "I wouldn't want to put it on casually," she explained. "I'm sort of saving myself for the right man."[7]

Feeder-feedee relationships are controversial, even among fat admirers. It is striking that the majority of feedees seem to be heterosexual women: fat lesbians who discussed the phenomenon in an issue of *FaT GiRL* were appalled by the patriarchal implications of a man fattening up a woman so that she remained totally dependent on him. But as Supersize Betsy herself points out, few male feeders are in fact willing to take their female feedees to immobility:

> There are other problems that come with the size, like skin-fold rashes. You'd have to be with somebody that's willing to care for you 24 hours a day. And those people don't really exist. I've been looking for six years and I haven't found any man who really wanted to take me to immobility. They may fantasize about it, but they don't really want to do it.[8]

It is this realm of fantasy that fat pornography caters to. And although fantasies are always intensely private experiences, one thing we do know about them is that they do not occur randomly. Instead, what people fantasize about is related to their position and power in the real world. For this reason, fantasies tend to cluster in socially predictable ways. So a sociological question that can be asked about fat fantasies is: Who has them?

If we begin with gender and sexuality, we can note that there are, perhaps unsurprisingly, no pornographic Web sites or magazines where five-hundred-pound men strut their ample stuff for women. Neither have I found much evidence of lesbian-oriented fat pornography. The zine *FaT GiRL*, which I have already mentioned, existed for three years in the mid-1990s, but it only published six issues and then stopped appearing in 1997. The images in *FaT GiRL* were in many ways similar to the images of display and eating that I have shown so far. There was more sex, however: the first issue contained a centerfold that featured a fat woman in leather being fisted in the vagina. This image was typical of the magazine. Whenever fat sex was portrayed in *FaT GiRL*, it tended to be bondage or sadomasochistic sex.

There are Web sites and magazines for large gay men, such as magazines called *Bulge* and *Bulk Male*, and a Web site called *Big Bellies*. These exhibit some of the same pictorial conventions as the magazines or Web sites that feature women: that is to say, there is a focus on the stomach, and there are sometimes photos of eating. But a very clear difference is that the extreme forms of obesity that characterize many of the "Big Beautiful Women" (BBW) Web sites and videos are absent. There are no five-hundred-pound gay male porn stars. Instead, gay male fat admiration seems focused on an ample, often hairy belly but not on disabling obesity. I have not found any indication that there are any fat gay men out there wanting to be taken to immobility by other men.

Race is a very interesting dimension of fat pornography, because fat pornography is consistently racially marked as white. There are, of course, hundreds of "booty" videos, magazines and Web sites in which black and Latina women display their behinds. But the kind of fat pornography I am discussing here consists overwhelmingly of white women, and it seems directed, as far as one can tell, at white men. It is not particularly obvious why this should be the case, especially when you consider that one of the most widespread and enduring images of fat women in North American culture is the black "mammy."

And sure enough, the mammy image was raised during a roundtable discussion on fatness and race that appeared in the third issue of *FaT GiRL*. During that conversation, an African American woman named Wolfie observed that she had always found that it's more acceptable for women of color to be fat "because we're the 'Earth Mothers,' we're more in touch with our 'naturalistic feelings.' . . ."

"Or [you're] Mammies," another woman interrupts.

Yeah, Wolfie agrees: "And it's like, No, you do not get to automatically take comfort from my tits!"[9]

The kinds of associations between black women, "naturalistic feelings," and large breasts that "automatically" offer comfort are, of course, the result of a long and demeaning racist history. So why aren't they out there circulating in fat pornography? It's surprising that they're not, because while it holds much allure for many, pornography is the last place one should look to find socially progressive messages. To the contrary, pornography is the corner to which the politically incorrect retreats where it has nowhere else to go. Pornography welcomes the forbidden. It sustains the vulgar. It traffics in the offensive. Hence, the fact that fat pornography has not (yet?) exploited racist images of obese black women is puzzling.

Perhaps the place to find an explanation for this absence is in social attitudes toward obesity. To the extent that Wolfie's experiences can be generalized, it seems that perhaps (in the United States, at any rate) fatness in nonwhite women may not elicit the same condemnation as does fatness in white women. This is certainly the case in many nonwhite communities, where we know that fatness does not have the same strong associations with revulsion that it has among whites. Studies about body images among different groups conclude that among African Americans, for example, there is a more flexible image of female beauty—one that places more emphasis on personal style than on approximations to an ideal standard.[10] We might say that the reason why fat pornography is a predominantly white genre is this: because fatness in women of color isn't as denied and repressed as fatness in white women is, black fat doesn't lend itself as readily to pornographic representation.

So, What's with the Eating?

Why does fat pornography exist at all? Like all pornography, fat pornography produces *frissons* (little eruptions of surprise, shock, and/or erotic pleasure) because it transgresses social norms. It celebrates what society tells us is nasty. And the way pornography celebrates is by inverting social messages: turning them on their head. In fat pornography, what is inverted, obviously, is the value that society places on thin bodies and on the carefully controlled eating strategies we should all practice in order to attain those bodies. Celebrating fat as sexy is an outrageous provocation in a society where fat women are reviled. *FaT GiRL* asked readers how they thought fat women were represented in the media. A typical response was this:

> *Hatefully. You almost never see positive representations of fat women on TV. If a woman is fat, she has to be: sloppy, ugly, funny—but self-deprecating funny, asexual, confined to her home or office, sitting in front of the TV eating bon bons, on a diet, on an exercise binge, sick because she's got high blood pressure or she's fat (not because she's sick from dieting, purging and yo-yoing to meet some impossible standard), hoping for Mr. Right to love her in spite of her "weight problem."*[II]

On the other hand, examples of the outright celebration of women who shed pounds abound. The adulation that greets celebrities like Elizabeth Hurley and Catherine Zeta-Jones when they manage to lose the weight they gain during pregnancy is of the ecstatic sort usually reserved for Olympic champions. Many seemed to think that the actress Renée Zellweger deserved an Oscar in 2003 simply because she transformed herself from the overweight frump she portrayed in *Bridget Jones's Diary* into the svelte sexpot she played in *Chicago*. Oprah Winfrey's never-ending "battles" with her weight (for an earlier generation, it was Elizabeth Taylor's) continue to galvanize a nation. Ex–Spice Girl Geri Halliwell keeps getting thinner and blonder and has built a second career out of dieting. The cover of the second installment of her autobiography features her smugly entwined in a tape measure.

In contemporary Western societies, where fat is relentlessly demonized as unattractive, unhealthy, and undesirable, it is both culturally and psychologically predictable that there should be a "return of the repressed." Long ago, Freud explained that a surefire way to make something desirable is to say it is bad and forbid it. We see evidence of this all the time. What words do small children positively delight in repeating? The forbidden, "bad" ones. What do we do to celebrate some victory or happy event? We eat cake, drink alcohol, smoke cigars—all behaviors that are widely classified as "bad" and that many people ban in their day-to-day lives.

Because the forbidden incites desire *because it is forbidden*, to wonder why fat pornography exists is to miss the obvious, at least if you believe Freud. He would tell us that it exists, not despite the fact that it repels many, but precisely *because* it repels many people.

The much more intriguing thing to consider is what exactly we are seeing when we see fat pornography. If it is indeed the case, as cultural critic Laura Kipnis puts it, that "fat . . . is what

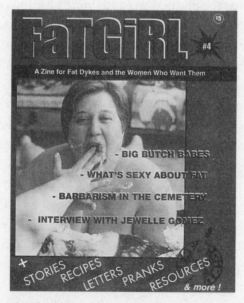

Photo by Vicki Markin. Reproduced with permission

our culture doesn't want to look at. Pornography, in response, puts it on view," then what exactly is it that is on view?[12] What are we being called upon to see when we watch a video of 350-pound Sandie enjoying a playful experience with a large bowl of whipped cream, or when we gaze at 540-pound Supersize Betsy eating a huge breakfast in bed in the nude? Or when we see this happy lesbian on the cover of *FaT GiRL*?[13]

One of the first scholarly studies of hard-core pornographic films was written by Linda Williams, a professor of film studies at the University of California, Berkeley. Williams's book, *Hard Core*, was published in 1989;[14] today it is regarded as a classic. The central claim of *Hard Core* is that pornography poses a challenge for itself that it subsequently has problems resolving. The challenge is how to depict true sexual pleasure. Men's pleasure is easy to show. It is hard if not impossible for a man to fake an ejaculation, especially given the low budgets and limited editing capacities of most pornographic films. Hence, the so-called *money shot*—the orgasmic scene at the end of a sexual encounter where a man ejaculates onto a woman's body or face—says it all, which is why those shots exist in the first place. In other words, the coitus interruptus we see in porn films is not a magnanimous gesture of the industry to help prevent unwanted pregnancies among pornographic actresses. It is there to show that the sex that is depicted is genuine, hot, and orgasmic. For the man.

Women's sexual pleasure is much trickier to portray convincingly. Sure, a woman can moan and writhe and cry, "I'm coming, I'm coming." But how do you know for sure that she *really* had an orgasm and that she isn't just acting or faking it? Where is the evidence? For a long time, pornography dealt with this problem either by ignoring it (pre-1970s stag films, for example, were indifferent to women's orgasms) or else by portraying a woman's invisible pleasure by showing close-ups of a man's visible ejaculation. The single most famous scene in which this occurs is the climactic sequence in the 1972 film *Deep Throat*, when the star, Linda Lovelace, has her "first" orgasm. The entire movie builds up to this moment, and it finally occurs when Linda Lovelace performs fellatio on a doctor who has diagnosed her as having a clitoris at the back of her throat. In the film, Linda Lovelace's orgasm is visually represented by big bells ringing, fireworks exploding, a rocket launching—and the doctor ejaculating onto her cheek. We don't see the doctor's face during this orgasmic sequence. All the visual signs represent her pleasure; the camera remains focused on Linda Lovelace's face, even during the climactic money shot.

During the past few decades, pornography has attempted to find other ways of depicting female pleasure. Some films occasionally omit money shots: they emphasize foreplay and afterplay, and they film sex acts in full figure, rather than zooming in on close-ups of genitals. But despite these innovations, visually depicting female sexual pleasure continues to be a specter that haunts pornography as a representational genre. How can female pleasure be represented as anything but desire for or submission to a penis that symbolizes phallic power and potency?

This is where fat pornography suddenly becomes very interesting. In its own modest way, fat pornography may have hit on one powerful way of providing another representation of female pleasure.

Shortly before he died in 1984, the French philosopher Michel Foucault granted an interview in which he waxed lyrical about sadomasochistic sex. Foucault had discovered S/M a few years earlier and was captivated, partly because of the sexual charge it gave him, but also because the philosopher in him perceived S/M as something truly radical. Foucault had spent the better part of his working life documenting the rise of sexuality in Western life. He had shown that what we consider to be "sexuality" is not a natural or God-given phenomenon but is, instead, a culturally and historically specific way of linking together particular body parts, specific activities, sensations, and knowledges. For example, in contemporary mainstream understandings, sex is widely thought to be activity of limited duration that occurs when a person's so-called erogenous zones (nipples, mouth, genitals) are stimulated, ideally to orgasm, often by coming into contact with another person's erogenous zones. This activity is supposed to be pleasurable and to produce pleasure, and its most socially sanctioned forms occur between persons of roughly equal age, class background, and status.

Sadomasochistic sex disregards many of these linkages and rearranges them. In S/M sex, objects and body parts that are not usually imagined to be sexual (clothespins, dog collars, urine, fists) become highly eroticized. S/M sex often does not result in orgasm for anyone involved. Although it is pleasurable, it arrives at pleasure through pain, thereby linking together two sensations that "sexuality" tells us are supposed to be kept apart. It exaggerates and eroticizes power in situations where "sexuality" exhorts us to equalize or downplay it. Foucault became fascinated by S/M because he saw it as breaking with the regime that "sexuality" has imposed on our bodies, our relationships, and our perceptions of pleasure. If "sexuality" is one of the ways we come to know ourselves as individuals in contemporary society ("I am straight," "I am gay"), then S/M sex, with its disaggregation of bodies, pleasures, and knowledges, offers refreshing and subversive ways of knowing ourselves in different ways, in ways that may lead to different potentials and realizations.

Had Foucault lived long enough to surf the Web and light upon some of the "Big Beautiful Women" home pages, I think he would have liked fat pornography for similar reasons. Like sadomasochistic sex, fat pornography displaces erotic pleasure from the genitals and disperses it to other parts of the body, thereby reconfiguring what can count as a pleasurable body. That both S/M sex and fat pornography do this makes the equation in *FaT GiRL* between fat women and S/M a logical one.

Another break that fat pornography accomplishes is with the limited time frame that "sexuality" demands. Our understanding of sexuality dictates that we should not have sex all the time. Sex should occur in private, away from public view, and for limited periods of time (twenty minutes, two hours, a whole afternoon . . . but not all the time). Fat pornography flouts this convention. It does not restrict itself to portraying particular, temporally discrete acts: indeed, to the extent that eating is sexy and even pornographic, then five-hundred-pound-plus women like Supersize Betsy clearly have bodies marked by a long history of pleasure—pleasure that far exceeds the limited duration of any particular act of sex. Sex here is not an act or a series of acts so much as it is a deliberately fashioned kind of *self*—an insistent sexualized self that does not stay behind closed doors but that unapologetically broadcasts its pleasure at every moment of every day.

Finally, despite the fact that most of it seems designed for male consumption, there is a decidedly nonphallic component to fat pornography's representations of female pleasure. In fact, if we wanted, we could continue to get all French about this and argue that fat pornography is a representation of the what psychoanalyst Jacques Lacan, in characteristically cryptic language, called the "*jouissance* of ~~The~~ Woman." *Jouissance* is French for pleasure, or orgasm. And Lacan crossed out the *The* to indicate that there is no such thing as "The Woman," even though one of psychoanalysis's favorite pastimes has always been to generalize about "The Woman" and lecture us about what "She" wants. Toward the end of his long life, Lacan finally concluded that psychoanalysis had misperceived women all along. Female pleasure, he decided, is actually not dependent on, or even really desirous of, the phallus. On the contrary, what characterizes female pleasure and sets it apart from male pleasure is precisely that it exceeds and bypasses the phallus, therefore undermining its imagined role as the ultimate bestower of rapture.

Fat pornography depicts just this. There is no sense in many of the images that circulate in fat porn that the thing that is going to save the day for the models is a man's penis, or any other kind of genital sex. There is no indication that they are fantasizing about performing fellatio when they eat their hamburgers or that they long to be penetrated as they enjoy their stacks of breakfast pancakes. The position of the phallus is usurped here by food.

There is another French psychoanalyst—this one a feminist, expelled from Lacan's institute precisely for that reason (this was before Lacan grew old and ended up becoming something of a feminist himself). Luce Irigaray has made much in her writing about the power that a woman's "two lips" might have to *parler femme* (speak woman) and thereby displace the male phallus from its Freudian throne as the supposed source of all erotic joy. The "two lips" Irigaray refers to are vaginal lips. But maybe we should, instead, consider those other two lips and what they can do. And perhaps those intensely mouthy pleasures of lapping, licking, slurping, and crunching that we see depicted in fat pornography are some version of *parler femme*—a language of pleasure, power, and supreme disinterest in everything the phallus has to offer.

Heavenly

Lena Gemzöe

In northern Portugal, not far from the Atlantic coast, there is a little village called Balasar. Balasar looks like many other villages in the Portuguese countryside: simple stone houses on tiny plots of land clustered together around a church. Goats tug at the grass just beside the main road. Their jingling bells fill the air with brittle clanging. Only the church bells, marking the passing hours of the day, ring louder. At the village's tavern a few guests eat in silence, virtually hidden under the vine leaves that shade the terrace. For a tourist, there appears to be nothing in particular to see or to do in Balasar. And yet almost every day, all year round, Balasar receives visitors from places all over Portugal and even from abroad.

These visitors usually head straight for the church. They walk up to a particular tombstone located inside the church, and they stop there and pray for a few minutes. When they are finished, they are escorted through a little alley to one of the old stone houses close to the church. They reverently inspect every detail of the simple furnishings of the house. Finally, they are allowed to enter a bedroom that is large enough for only one person at a time.

On an austere wooden bed there is a white nightgown that has been carefully arranged on the sheets. At first glance it looks as though it is draped over the body of a woman. It isn't, but resting on the pillow just above the collar of the gown is a life-size photograph of a woman's smiling face. Even though it is only a photo, one immediately notices the woman's radiant eyes. This is what the visitors have come to see. They crowd in the doorway to see "the lady" in the bed, waiting for their turn to enter the room. They fall to their knees before the image in the bed, and mouth a silent prayer.

The lady whom the pilgrims to Balasar worship is known familiarly by her first name, Alexandrina. Alexandrina was an ordinary peasant girl born in Balasar in 1904. She lived in the same modest house her entire life. Her fame in Portugal is based on a curious fact: during the final thirteen years of her life, Alexandrina lived without eating anything but the thin white wafer, the Eucharist, that Catholics receive when they take Holy Communion.

I heard about Alexandrina of Balasar for the first time when I was living in Vila Branca, a nearby town, writing a book about religion.[1] I was fascinated by the stories people told me about their devotion to the Virgin Mary and the local saints of northern Portugal. I was also able to join my Portuguese friends on their pilgrimages to the many saints' shrines in the region. When I first heard about Saint Alexandrina, who had helped and cured many people, I was confused. Saint Alexandria was not a Christian martyr who had died hundreds of years ago, who people had only heard about through legends. She had been an ordinary Portuguese woman, and I knew several people in Vila Branca who had actually met her before her death in 1955. They told me how they had entered the tiny bedroom in the house at Balasar and gazed into Alexandrina's eyes—eyes which, they said, glowed with a celestial light. When I, the skeptical anthropologist, asked them how they knew that Alexandrina really was a saint, their answer was simple: Alexandrina's body, a body that could survive for over a decade without sustenance, was the proof.

Naturally I had difficulty believing that someone could live for so long without eating. But what I could not doubt was that the people in Vila Branca who had visited Alexandrina were convinced that they had met a living saint.

Saint Alexandrina's renunciation of food elevated her and made her holy. This connection between the absence of fat and the presence of divinity is startling: How can the ability to live without eating become a sign of holiness? And what are the religious dimensions of eating, food, and fat?

Saint Alexandrina of Balasar

Alexandrina of Balasar was not the only woman in northern Portugal who became holy by not eating, although she is the most famous. There are a number of known cases of young women who have achieved saintly status by remaining alive despite permanently fasting. The Portuguese anthropologist Joao de Pina-Cabral has labeled these women "non-eaters."[2] These non-eaters have a number of characteristics in common: they are all young girls of rural origin, they are sexually pure, and they begin their fasting around the onset of adolescence. In addition, their rejection of "ordinary" food is accompanied by an intense focus on "holy" food, the ritual of Holy Communion.

The Catholic hierarchy does not recognize the non-eaters as saints. On the contrary, the Church does everything in its power to discourage the cults that develop around non-eaters. But try as it might, in some cases the Church does not succeed in stamping these cults out. And if a cult continues to grow and attract devotees, the Church might be forced to acknowledge it. All of this is precisely what happened with the cult of Alexandrina.[3]

Alexandrina's full name was Alexandrina Maria da Costa. At the age of fourteen, she, her sister, and one other young woman were chased by three men. The young women hid in Alexandrina's house. Fearing rape, Alexandrina jumped out of a window in order to escape. During the next five years she gradually became paralyzed from the injuries she sustained from the fall. By the age of twenty-one she was confined to bed. In the stories the Church now tells about her life, this incident is taken as a proof of Alexandrina's virtuous character: it was in order to safeguard her sexual purity that she embarked upon the life of saintliness.

Some years after Alexandrina's confinement to bed, Jesus appeared to her and announced that she had been chosen for a life of suffering in order to save human souls. She started to have mystical experiences such as religious ecstasy, visions, stigmata, and pains that resembled the sufferings of the crucified Christ. The most salient mark of her holiness, however, and the one that gave her popular reputation of sanctity, was the state of permanent fasting in which she lived during the last thirteen years of her life.

Although there were skeptics, among ordinary people, Alexandrina's reputation for holiness grew larger as her body grew thinner. The religious establishment, however, rejected her. Priests accused Alexandrina of fooling naive believers. The doctors who regularly examined her did everything they could to prove that she was a charlatan. Some declared that Alexandrina's religious visions and stigmata were the result of hysteria. They claimed that she was not really fasting—her sister or mother must be feeding her on the sly.

Alexandrina found the continuous medical examinations to which she was subjected painful and humiliating. However, to put an end to the controversy, she agreed to be hospitalized in the city of Porto for forty days. During this time, she would be under constant medical supervision. She agreed to this on the condition that she would be given the sacrament of Holy Communion once a day. The medical establishment was excited by the scientific challenge her case presented. The doctors hoped to either reveal Alexandrina as a con artist or else to find some kind of scientific explanation for how she could remain alive eating only the Host. But at the end of the forty days, the doctors had to acknowledge that there were no natural causes that could explain Alexandrina's survival. When her slight body was taken from the hospital, an enthusiastic crowd of devotees greeted her.

The Church, however, did not give up. In 1944, the archbishop of northern Portugal appointed an ecclesiastical commission to examine Alexandrina. This commission concluded that her religious visions and ecstasy were caused by neurosis and wishful thinking. The messages she allegedly received from Christ were officially declared inauthentic. The archbishop pronounced a ban on further public discussion of the issue. He furthermore decreed that the Catholic clergy should suppress all information about Alexandrina, and ordered the priest of Balasar to ensure that public visits to Alexandrina's house ceased.

Alexandrina herself was threatened with the withdrawal of Holy Communion, her only form of sustenance, if she contested the archbishop's orders.

During the years that followed, some priests raised their voices in defense of Alexandrina, while others submitted to the archbishop. In the end, the efforts of the Church to dissolve the popular cult of Alexandrina were in vain. Stories spread by the people Alexandrina had cured encouraged a steady flow of pilgrims to her bedside. No pilgrim who visited her left disappointed. Alexandrina listened to every worry, instance of bad luck, misfortune, or sinful behavior that people told her about. She gained a reputation for being able to see into people's hearts and know exactly what they needed. Even the most stubborn nonbeliever was said to have returned to the faith after seeing Alexandrina.

By the beginning of the 1950s, Alexandrina sometimes received more than one hundred visitors per day. Overwhelmed by this popular adulation, the archbishop withdrew his prohibition to visit her. Since her death in 1955, the Church has reevaluated Alexandrina's case, and in 1983 the first step of the official process of her sanctification was taken. The woman who has long been a saint in the eyes of the people is finally on her way to becoming a saint in the eyes of the Church.

The Road to Sanctity

Alexandrina of Balasar constitutes a contemporary example of what religious historians have described as a particularly *female* pursuit of holiness.[4] There are of course both holy men as well as holy women in the Catholic Church, and both men and women have practiced fasting and abstinence. Nevertheless, there is a distinct gender difference in the emphasis on food and fasting, a difference that becomes especially clear in the period from the twelfth to the fifteenth centuries. Whereas men who entered monasteries or wrote about the spiritual life were more preoccupied with the renunciation of wealth and power as a means of holiness, women, who usually had little wealth or power to renounce in the first place, were more prone to emphasize food—or, rather, the absence of food—in their spirituality.

These women's emphasis on food is linked to the fact that food has been a resource that women could control. As mothers, women often had the obligation to distribute food to their families before they themselves could eat. Nuns would distribute food to the poor in acts of charity, and renounce food for themselves. This kind of renunciation became a powerful way for pious women to express their devotion to the Church.

Renouncing food has also been perceived as a means of renouncing sexual desire. In the history of Christianity, fasting has been interpreted as a means of sealing the body against sex. In this sense, the rejection of food practiced by medieval women could be seen as an expression of an unwillingness to be pushed into marriage and childbirth. In the case of Alexandrina of Balasar, the connection between food, sexuality, and subordination is somewhat different but still clear. The jump out the window, described by the Church as a proof of her virtuous character, was in fact a desperate action taken in order to avoid being raped. One of the three men who pursued Alexandrina was her former patron, a man who had treated her badly and forced her to perform dangerous and exhausting work in spite of her tender age. Alexandrina's mother took her daughter out of the patron's service, claiming that he had broken the contract. The assault was revenge on the girl for complaining to her mother. In a very concrete sense, then, Alexandrina's "choice" of the road to sanctity was made in fear and protest against abuse at the hands of a man.

There are so many reports of mediaeval women fasting with such severity that scholars speak in terms of "holy anorexia"—sometimes with doubts about whether the fasting should be seen as holy or as an obsessive-compulsive personality disorder. The holy anorexia of these saints does have some things in common with the contemporary phenomenon of anorexia.

Researchers and doctors do not agree about which particular combination of psychological, social, and medical factors seem to lie behind contemporary anorexia. But one thing unites different explanations: the issue of control. Young girls come to feel that in a frightening and uncontrollable world, at least they can exert a control over their own body fat. This interpretation corresponds with the feminist viewpoint that anorexia, which often begins around adolescence, is a way of refusing to enter female adulthood, which is perceived—rightly, feminists argue—as a subordinated condition. Anorexia results in dramatically reduced body fat, leading to the cessation of menstruation. In this sense, the illness becomes a real rejection of motherhood. With the reproductive capacity suspended, and with the absence of breasts, which don't develop on young anorexics, the emaciated anorectic body can be seen as the reverse image of the pregnant female body, with its swelling breasts and belly. Like secular anorexics, non-eaters initiate their fasting on the cusp between being girls and becoming women. Instead of preparing for courtship and marriage, they become saints.

Contemporary anorexia has been seen as a consequence of the lifestyle of Western women, in which diets and physical exercise are the norm. In such a context, the disease can be seen to be at least partly brought on by the pressures to live up to a distorted feminine body ideal. In rural Portugal, the social context is different. Until the 1990s, diets were not part of young girls' lifestyles there. When Alexandrina grew up at the beginning of the twentieth century, people in the poor rural countryside of Portugal found it difficult to put enough food on the table each day. During long periods, many families lived only on what they could harvest from their small plots of land, and only occasionally did they have access to rich, fatty foods like meat. In such a context fat was valued and diets were unimaginable.

So although there are clearly parallels between the secular anorexics and non-eaters, there are also differences. Another crucial one is that the fasting of the non-eater is combined with an intense participation in the ritual of Holy Communion. The religious mysticism elaborated on by Alexandrina of Balasar is very similar to that of a much earlier non-eater saint named Alpaïs. In one official account of her life, dating from the late twelfth century, the Virgin Mary tells Alpaïs:

> *Because, dear sister, you bore long starvation in humility and patience, in hunger and thirst, without any murmuring, I grant you now to be fattened with an angelic and spiritual food. And as long as you are in this little body, corporeal food and drink will not be*

necessary for the sustaining of your body, nor will you hunger for
bread or any other food . . . because after you have once tasted the
celestial bread and drunk of the living fountain you will remain
fattened for eternity.[5]

The emaciated bodies of the saints in this world will be fattened in the next, according to this account. The Blessed Virgin's words make it clear that holy fasting involves a distinction between ordinary food and celestial, or heavenly, nourishment. Non-eaters like Alexandrina or Alpaïs reject all ordinary food, but they enthusiastically consume the wafer that symbolizes the body of Christ in the Eucharistic ritual. Alexandrina of Balasar received Holy Communion at least once a week from the priest who was also her spiritual counselor, but during some periods she received it as often as once a day. It was always extremely hard for her to endure not receiving the wafer. This could happen if the village priest was away or did not have time to come to her house and give her the sacrament. On these occasions the Church now claims that Christ would come to her in a vision and give her Holy Communion himself.

When the body of a woman is fed only on the Eucharist, at a certain point it ceases to be an ordinary human body. Instead, the woman's body becomes like the body of Christ. Feeding on God's body, it becomes divine.[6] This road to holiness makes the power dimension of these ascetic practices especially clear. Throughout history, the Catholic Church has reserved its positions of spiritual leadership for men. As late as 1994, Pope John Paul II restated that women must be prohibited from ordination into the priesthood. He furthermore proclaimed that this teaching was to be "definitively held," which is ecclesiastical language for "End of discussion."[7]

But despite the fact that women cannot become ordained as priests in the Catholic Church and, hence, cannot ascend the ranks of Church hierarchy, there is a road to spiritual authority that has always been open to women throughout the history of Christianity. That road is sainthood.

As saints, holy women have always exerted a considerable influence over both religious and secular matters. Bridget of Sweden and Teresa of Ávila founded or reformed convents. Catherine of Siena, perhaps the most famous non-eater, was deeply concerned with the Church, and she intervened personally and frequently in the power struggles between popes during the papal schism of the late 1300s, when for forty years the Catholic Church had two competing popes. Like Catherine, many holy women did not hesitate to castigate bishops, popes, and even kings. (Bridget, for example, is famous for her intrigues against King Magnus II Eriksson of Sweden).

Moreover, holy women all gave their spiritual and theological opinions without formal education or official positions. The writings of women mystics such as Hildegard von Bingen or Julian of Norwich have enriched Christianity with a female theological tradition—despite the fact that women were not, for many centuries, officially allowed to interpret the Scriptures.

Compared with women like Catherine of Siena or Hildegard von Bingen, the power of a local modern-day saint such as Alexandrina of Balasar should perhaps not be overstated. But neither should it be underestimated or dismissed. During her lifetime, Alexandrina was a spiritual adviser to a large number of devotees, she distributed large sums of money to charity, and she freely dispensed her opinion on the religious matters of her time—all of this from her sickbed in her home at Balasar.

The Gluttonous Saint

The holiness of the non-eaters is based on the Christian tradition's opposition between sex and food as sensuous and sinful, and the renunciation of food and sex as holy. The Church prescribes fasting and sexual abstinence as a means of getting closer to God, and those individuals—like priests or holy women—who live their entire life in God's service should uphold these ideals with more vigor than other people. It is their ability to live more virtuously than the rest of us that gives holy individuals moral authority and power. A non-eater like Alexandrina achieved a position with considerable religious power. Non-eaters are believed to be able to recognize any immorality in the priest who gives her the communion wafer, something that implies that the non-eater is holier than a priest. The non-eater thus competes with the priest to establish who is holier. It is therefore easy to understand why non-eaters might be seen as a threat to the Catholic hierarchy, as Alexandrina was during her lifetime.

During my stay in the town of Vila Branca in the early 1990s, my friends invited me to go on a pilgrimage to visit another non-eater in the same region. I was excited to go, as this non-eater was actually alive. A visit to her, I thought, would perhaps reveal more of the secrets of the divine power of these saints. The non-eater was called "the little girl of Arouca," and according to my Portuguese friends she was a beautiful saint, thin and holy. Many residents in Vila Branca had gone to see her, and stories of her powers circulated throughout the region. As with Alexandrina, the Church disapproved of this popular devotion.

The little girl of Arouca lived in a small stone house, where she received her visitors. When we arrived at her house, members of her family directed us to her bed. It turned out that the "little girl" was a woman in her twenties. Her black hair framed her pale face, unadorned by makeup. She looked as though she were lying on her sickbed: her face was inexpressive; she did not even smile at the visitors.

The pilgrims were allowed to pass by the girl's bed, to ask her questions or make requests, and to give her monetary offerings. Most of them were too shy to approach her, and she only nodded to those who did. The whole atmosphere of this encounter with the living saint was somber and pious.

As soon as we came out of the house, though, one of the elderly women who had visited the saint before declared that the saint appeared fatter than the last time she saw her. (As a matter of fact, she did seem a little chubby—quite far from the emaciated look one would expect from someone living only on a single wafer taken once a day or once a week.)

I later realized that the pilgrims' comments on leaving the house were similar to other stories that I came to hear about the "little girl" of Arouca. These stories all suggested that the saint secretly gorged herself with food, and that her holy status had been used to enrich herself and her family. One of my woman friends who had visited the saint before recounted a telling story: a pilgrim loitering behind after the other pilgrims had left said he saw the little girl of Arouca reach down under her bed to remove a hidden plate of sausages and bacon, which she greedily, hurriedly, gobbled up before the next group of pilgrims arrived at her bedside.

The saintly "little girl" in stories like these is described not just as surreptitiously nibbling on a cracker or a piece of fruit, but as stuffing herself with really *fat* food: foods like sausages that are the ultimate transgression of the religious fasting prescribed by the Church.

A story like this provokes incredulous laughter in the villages, and is similar to the stories about priests that circulate in Portugal: scratch a priest's devout exterior, people joke, and you will find a cesspool of carnal depravity. Joking stories like these—told, I should emphasize, by people who devoutly believe in the power of priests and non-eaters—are ways of reconciling the power of holy individuals with the fact that they are, in essence, no different from "ordinary" women and men. Beneath the holy surface of the non-eater or the priest, there lurks the desires of ordinary women and men.

The fasting of the non-eaters evokes stories of the pleasures of eating and the sin of gluttony. The inversions involved in these stories show us how the idea of the non-fat as holy gains its meaning from the contrary idea of the fat as non-holy or even sinful. Stories of gluttonous saints with their mouths full of sausages are scandalous and funny because they build on a juxtaposition between the holy and the non-holy. They are also funny because a story of a "non-eater" who lies in her bed stuffing herself with fat calls forth an image of the truly unthinkable: a fat female saint.

Because they are women in the Christian tradition, non-eaters have been excluded from any kind of official spiritual authority. Instead, they have gained authority through personal characteristics, charisma, and a religiosity expressed though their bodies. A non-eater succeeds in transforming her own body into a divine object, worthy of the worship and devotion of pilgrims. In the cult of a non-eater, it is a living female body, a body without fat, which exudes its sacred power.

The cult of non-eaters is ultimately based on the idea of the fat-free female body as holy. It is this kind of body—one that is desiccated and hard—that exerts its spiritual magnetism on the pilgrims. In this way, pilgrimage sites like Arouca and Balasar express in a powerful way a message that has remained true for women over the centuries: Reject the fat of this world, that you may become fattened for eternity.

 Talk

Fanny Ambjörnsson

"Fy Faaaaan!" screams Anna, using the vulgar Swedish expression for stomach-churning disgust. "Look at my upper arms! Look! Look how they wobble! It's gross!"

Anna is leaning with her back pressed against her school locker. She is wearing a sleeveless shirt, and she lifts up her bare arms for her girlfriends, who gather closer to see.

The girls glance at Anna's arms, but instead of pitying her, they respond with a chorus of their own imperfections. "Thick" thighs, "fat" bellies, "heavy" butts, "double" chins, "loose" love handles: every one of Anna's friends has something, some short-coming of her own, to chime in with. And as they all stand there next to Anna's locker, their voices begin to overlap and blend, turning what began as a command to look at Anna's arms into a kind of mournful madrigal of feminine defects.

As this chorus is being sung, another girl, Marlene, is walking down the hall. Everyone can see that Marlene's hair is wet. She looks clean and fresh and newly scrubbed, as if she has just stepped out of the shower. And indeed she has: as Marlene walks past the little lamenting group, she says hello to the girls and lets it drop that she has just come from the gym. There is a short moment of silence. "Wow," murmurs Julia in a jealous whisper. Mia announces that she hasn't worked out at the gym in four days. "I really get stressed about things like this," she tells everyone. "If I don't work out every second day I get anxious, 'cause I have to work out to feel good. I guess I was born fat!"

I spent the better part of a year in the company of girls like Anna and Mia and Julia, all of whom are young Swedish teen-agers in their junior year in high school. I hung out with the girls in school, tagged along when they cut class, danced with them at parties, and had long conversations with them in the lunch-room, on the subway, and in their bedrooms, listening to the latest Swedish and American pop—all in an attempt to under-stand what it is like being a teenage girl these days in a country like Sweden, where women have more political power than any-where else in the world.

Sweden is a country where women make up 43 percent of the national parliament (compared to a paltry 18 percent in Britain and 14 percent in the United States Congress); where the cur-rent minister of defense is a woman; where federally financed day-care centers for children are universal; where maternity-leave benefits are the most generous in the world; where women make up a larger percentage of the labor force than any other country; and where feminist ideals play an important role in policy decisions and the day-to-day running of the country.

Yet, as it turns out, female representation in the parliament or the labor force, the gender of the minister of defense, and feminist ideas about day-care centers or maternity leave don't rate very high on the scale of what Swedish teenage girls talk about. What does capture their attention is fat. Fat is spoken about constantly. Yet, it is only ever spoken about in one way: in disgusted tones and with appalled inflections. Fat of all kinds is detested: greasy food, oily hair, a fat woman on the subway, plump thighs—all are objects of horror. But most disturbing for the girls is the idea that fat is not entirely external. On the contrary, fat is something they harbor inside their own bodies. The fat is in there somewhere, nesting, malevolent, biding its time. This evil invisible fat causes great distress. Virtually every single girl I met, no matter how svelte, no matter how popular, no matter how pretty, expressed dissatisfaction with her body.

This likely comes as no surprise. In the popular imagination, the teenage girl is someone who is almost pathologically preoccupied with her own appearance and body size. She is a victim: a deluded soul who desperately tries to embody an impossible feminine ideal. She is a sad dupe who sits for hours in front of the mirror, perhaps surrounded by a cluster of similarly duped female friends, all obsessed with the size of their waistlines and the shades of their eye shadow.

While this stereotype is obviously exaggerated, it is not entirely inaccurate. Since the 1980s, feminist scholars in Sweden, the United States, and elsewhere have provided ample documentation of the insecurities and doubts that afflict young girls in Western societies.[1] The insecurities have a number of sources, but one that is crucial is, of course, the relentless exposure to the kind of body that one continually sees in advertisements and the mass media—a body that weighs 23 percent less than the average woman (a generation ago, the gap was only 8 percent).[2] Scholars have suggested that the pressure to approximate these ideal bodies leads increasing numbers of women to eating disorders or to "body distortion disorder," a kind of psychosis that drives an individual to seek ever increasing amounts of cosmetic surgery in order to feel attractive.

All of this is deplorable, clearly. But instead of just joining in with all the commentators who bemoan the plight of unconfident, victimized women, I wonder whether there might not be a different way of looking at body images among girls. What would happen if we looked, not just at what individual girls think about their bodies, but at the way they actually talk about their bodies together with other girls? What would we see if we examined the effects of girls' talk about fat—if we looked at what the talk about fat *does* among the girls? How does talk about fat organize and regulate social bonds and relations between girls?

Someone opens with a negative comment about her "fat" body and another answers along the same lines. This might seem like a banal, innocent interaction. But a closer inspection reveals that this kind of exchange is possible only because girls have learned when, with whom, and in what way they can discuss fat. This is not obvious or easily acquired knowledge. In fact, speaking about fat always involves skill and delicacy—a kind of balancing act.

During a lunch break, Julia, who was generally regarded as one of the prettier girls in the class, tells me and the group of girls sitting with her that she has been really naughty. "I haven't been to the gym for at least a week," she confesses. The other girls shake their heads and protest: "No, Julia, don't worry," they tell her. "You don't have to work out: you are thin enough as you are."

While other girls are telling Julia how thin she is, Andrea leans her head toward her friend Malena, who is sitting next to her. Sighing, Andrea says to Malena, loudly enough for everyone to hear, that the two of them are probably the only girls in the class who really do need to go the gym, since they are both a bit overweight.

Hearing this, the other girls at the lunch table immediately stop talking. They look at Andrea, expressions of undisguised disapproval on their faces. Malena pulls away from Andrea and ignores her. Even though nobody actually comes right out and says so, it is clear that Andrea has committed a big fat faux pas. Her transgression is so serious that for some time she is more or less ostracized from the inner clique of the girls' group.

What did Andrea do wrong? We've already seen that girls talk about fat all the time. So what exactly was Andrea's mistake? The indiscretion was this: to refer to yourself as fat and in need of improvement is fine. But to tell another girl that she is as fat as you is a gaffe of almost cosmic proportions.

Andrea's blunder and the other girls' reactions to it suggest that fat talk is more complicated than it may appear at first glance. Andrea was attempting to join in the requisite fat talk, but her attempt to forge an alliance with one of the other girls by saying that they were both in need of the gym fell flat. Andrea did not wait for Malena to begin bemoaning her own body. Instead she jumped the gun. A girl can complain about how big *her* belly is, or how hopelessly fat *her* thighs have become. She can—indeed, she is expected to—belittle herself. And her friends can contribute to the conversation with enumerations of their own flaws. But to volunteer comments about someone else being fat—that is not friendship. It is, in fact, the opposite of friendship. It is what you say about people you hate.

In this respect, fat talk is not only talk about fat bodies. Instead, it is a way of establishing friendships with some girls and ostracizing others. Andrea missed—or maybe she just forgot—this crucial point. She was certainly not trying to hurt Malena when she commented on her friend's body. But she broke the golden rule of fat talk, which is: thou shalt not even hint that someone you like is fat, especially not if that girl is sitting right there beside you.

There is another rule of fat talk that all popular girls know. This rule is rather devious, and it has to do with one's own body size. It is this: to be able to talk successfully about your fat body, you cannot be fat yourself. Virtually none of the girls I knew who talked about fat were actually overweight. On the contrary, those who seemed most eager to speak about their fat bodies were usually the slimmest and most popular girls.

Tessa, regarded as one of the school's most attractive girls, once told me and two of her friends, "I'm really unhappy with every little bit of my body. Everything is too big." The other girls around her sighed in unison. Lisa shook her head and comforted Tessa by telling her that she was definitely not fat: "Look here instead." She pointed to her jeans. "Look at my thighs if you want to see something really fat!"

Contrast Tessa with Sofia, another girl who sometimes tried

to join in the talk about fat. Whenever Sofia expressed her unhappiness with her body size, she was met with silence. She received no encouraging comments whatsoever, and the sighs from the other girls that always followed Sofia's lamentations carried a message far different from the one conveyed by remarks evoked by Tessa's assertions of fatness. The main reason for this difference is that Sofia is indeed somewhat chubby. And this fact, in the complex social world these girls create, is reason enough for ignoring her. Even though she was not banished from the group entirely, the other girls treated Sofia as if her failed body size was contagious. They seemed afraid that their own bodies would expand if they empathized with her chubbiness.

We can see the same logic in a comment by Lina, another girl in the school. Lina once told me, in a worried whisper, that some people think she resembles a girl who is somewhat overweight. The terrible thing is, Lina confided, she had actually sat next to the fat girl on the first day of school. "It was really a mistake," she said. "I didn't know her at all. I just sat down. But since we sat together, people thought we were, like, really good friends." Lina was anxious about this because she knows that among girls, the company you keep reflects your own status and popularity. This means that being seen in the company of a fat person risks relegating you to a lower place in the social hierarchy. Lina was worried that accidentally sitting next to an unknown fat girl caused people to see a physical resemblance between them. Concerns like this make it difficult for overweight girls to make friends with anyone who is slim and popular.

Being overweight in itself does not automatically disqualify a girl from inner circles of friendship, but it does impose certain restrictions. Chief among these is this: if you are overweight, don't talk about trying to change your body. If you plan to diet, do it in silence, and don't ask other girls for advice. Even if other, non-overweight girls exchange tips on diets or workout techniques to get rid of fat, the fat girl cannot. She is excluded from such activities. Whenever the topic comes up, overweight girls are either ignored, or dispatched with meaningful glances.

One way of interpreting this phenomenon is that fat talk constitutes what the French sociologist Pierre Bourdieu has called symbolic capital.[3] Symbolic capital comprises the qualities or characteristics that you have to possess in order to be acknowledged as someone worth talking to or interacting with. Generally speaking, a person who sounds like Prince Charles has more symbolic capital than someone who speaks like Joe Pesci, especially if the topic of discussion is opera, architecture, or wine. A person who knows how to use terms like *inning* or *halfback* has more symbolic capital in the context of sports than someone who doesn't know his wicket from a hole in the ground.

In the case of Swedish teenagers' fat talk, the situation is ironic: you only have the symbolic capital—the ability to talk about fat—if you don't have that which you are talking about— namely, fat. In other words, if you have real fat, you can have no symbolic fat.

But since fat talk is a vital means through which these girls bond and form friendships, and since slim girls don't talk about fat with anyone who actually is fat, overweight girls are not allowed to participate in the conversations that consolidate social relationships.

In view of this intricate social organization of fat talk, the commonplace assumptions about the exploitation of female bodies in Western cultures and the claims that most young girls feel ashamed or dissatisfied with their bodies seem somewhat simplistic. Managing to talk about your body with the appropriate kind of discomfort may indeed express a deeply felt dissatisfaction—but it also secures you a place in a network of friends. While talk about dissatisfaction with their supposedly fat bodies may indeed to some extent be a reflection of real frustration, it is also more than that. Because the girls expect others to share similar concerns about their bodies, the experience of worrying about fat is normalized; it is something you face because you are a girl. Expressing dissatisfaction with one's body becomes, in this sense, an important way of performing one's identity as a girl.

One day, two representatives from Swedish Association for Sex Education (in Swedish, abbreviated as RFSU) visited the school I worked in to discuss issues about sex and relationships. (Sweden was the first country in the world to introduce mandatory sex education in schools, in 1955. Talk about sex and visits by organizations like RFSU are commonplace). To facilitate this discussion, the students were divided into two separate groups, girls in one and boys in the other. When I asked Kristina, the representative from RFSU, about this, she told me that boys are usually interested in sex, and girls more often want to discuss body image, self-confidence, and relationships.

We all formed our chairs into a circle. Kristina asked us to stand up if we agreed with the statements she was going to read aloud. Looking out over the thirteen girls in the circle, Kristina began: "Being happy with one's appearance is hard." Everyone stood up.

Kristina sighed. "I would've been happy if there had been

anyone left on a chair, but that's not common," she said. "So," she continued, resigned, "what's the thing you are most dissatisfied with?"

Julia answered without hesitating: "My body."

Caroline continued: "There are days when you are more or less happy with it. But never totally."

The other girls agreed.

At that point, however, Joanna said something unexpected.

"Don't you think," she wondered, "that the problem is that you have to always talk about how you have problems being fat? 'Cause if you didn't, people would find you cocky. So it's really easier to just go on complaining."

Joanna cut straight to the heart of my own understanding of the role of fat talk in the lives of girls. Klara once explained to me that the reason some of the girls did not like their classmate Christine is because she was too self-confident. "She seems *too* happy with the way she looks, and she doesn't complain like everybody else does," Klara told me. In other words, Christine risked becoming an object of derision solely because she did not express dissatisfaction with her body. She risked being seen as arrogant, like a boy. Boys, after all, don't have to manage fat talk, since it is socially acceptable for a boy to be cocky and self-confident. It is even expected, the same way that self-denigration is expected among girls.

What all this means is that whether or not a girl is truly dissatisfied with her body is beside the point when it comes to managing fat talk. Either way, she has to be able to talk the talk. In this respect, expressing dissatisfaction about one's own body operates as what anthropologist Mimi Nichter calls a "protective device"—a kind of verbal amulet that deflects the envious thoughts of other people, and, simultaneously, secures your status as a normal, socially competent girl.[4]

But fat talk also highlights often overlooked aspects of the nature of victimization. In public debate and in scholarly literature, young women have been highlighted as victims of the slender, unobtainable beauty ideal, and they are said to suffer from low self-esteem, vulnerability, and eating disorders. In fact, this is a relatively recent development. Before the 1970s, scholars, journalists, social commentators, and others didn't pay much attention to girls. Popular books and films about youth culture were usually about boys and their cars and motorcycles and music. To the extent that girls figured at all in these depictions of youth culture, they were there as the tag-along partners of their much more exciting boyfriends.

In the 1980s there was a shift in the way that girls were depicted in scholarly work and popular media. They appeared rather one-dimensionally, as individuals with problems. If earlier generations of commentators were uncertain of or unconcerned with what preoccupied girls in their day-to-day lives and conversations, today everyone seems to know what girls do: they obsess, mostly about fat. This normalization of dissatisfaction seems to be one result of the victimization discourse of the 1980s and '90s. These were the years when anorexia and other eating disorders were discovered among young women and highlighted relentlessly in newspapers, television shows, schools, clinics, and so on. Although much good has undoubtedly come of all that attention, the constant alarms that females were dissatisfied with their bodies appears to have ended up conveying the impression that dissatisfaction is a normal female state. At some point, talk about fat became talk about being a girl.

Even though a lot has changed over the past fifty years, especially in a country like Sweden, social demands that women look a particular way compel females of all ages to continually think about their bodies, whether they like it or not. And since bodies can be altered—with new haircuts, different clothes, diets, aerobic classes, cosmetic surgery—if you exert control over your body and change it, *or even if you talk about it in the right way*, you may feel as though you have a certain kind of power in the world. In this respect, we might see fat talk as a way of staking a claim, of making yourself visible and legitimate, of showing people that you have independence, individuality, and style. But at the same time, fat talk ironically signals the opposite: it indicates conformity.

Fat is what deconstructivist scholars call an "absent presence": it is present as talk only to the extent that it is doesn't actually materialize on people's bodies. Maintaining this balance—keeping fat both present in talk and absent on your body—makes all the difference between being seen as a successful girl or as a total social failure.

So, as a Swedish high school girl, you can and should chew the fat. But you should never, ever, swallow it.

Leaky

Don Kulick and Thaïs Machado-Borges

During the 1990s—a decade when over half the population of several countries officially became overweight, and when in the world as a whole more people became obese than malnourished—the only known group of people anywhere on earth to have grown thinner, other than famine victims, were rich Brazilian women in cities.[1]

What, one might wonder, is their secret? It could be that in addition to starving themselves and paying vast amounts of money for personal trainers, plastic surgery, and liposuctions, many rich Brazilian women also take diet medicines that they insist make them leak fat.

This essay is not about those leaky women. It is, instead, about middle-class women who want to be like them. It is about how fat in any society is never just about weight or health or looks. Instead, fat is a symbol, a mirror we can gaze into to glimpse the things society tells us are the fairest of them all—and the things society tells us are the grossest, least fair of them all. Looking closely at how people think about fat tells us a lot about how they think about the world in which they live. In this sense, a desire to leak fat is a desire to leak out more than fat, something other than fat, something else besides fat.

Fat That Flows

One hot summer afternoon on the southeastern coast of Brazil, in 1999, Thaïs was relaxing on the porch of her friend Thelma's summer house.

Thelma is a staff administrator in her late forties. She is tall and white, and has a full but by no means heavy figure. A glass of cold Brazilian beer in hand, Thelma had just brought up the topic of a new diet pill that was all the rage throughout Brazil.

"I'm dying to buy Flowcal," she said to her friend Maria, who was similarly equipped with a glass of beer. "I read that it is the only diet medicine that does not have side effects."*

Maria, a white secretary in her fifties with a figure similar to Thelma's, agreed: "I know! It really sounds wonderful," she said. "They say that once you start to take it, it has an immediate effect!"

The names of diet medicines and products presented in this chapter have been changed.

"It will be on sale in a few weeks," Thelma said. "But you know, I'm going to check and see if I can buy some of it now on the black market so I can start taking it right away. I read that it will cost about two hundred reals a box [about U.S. $150], and that one box only lasts a month."

"That's expensive," Maria said. "And you have to take it every day if you want it to work."

"But Flowcal dissolves the fat in your body," Thelma explained. "It doesn't let the body accumulate fat. So you eat normally but you get thinner."

"I know," Maria said, and she repeated what she had heard others say: "It alters something in the body so that it won't absorb fat. All fat is eliminated."

Now it was Angela, Maria's seventeen-year-old daughter, who enthused: "Is that true? God, I want to take some of these pills as well!"

Her mother cut her off. "No way, Angela. Can you imagine? At that price! The only one in this family who is going to take it is me."

Thaïs sat with these women on the porch cradling her own glass of beer, trying hard to disguise her amazement at the intensity with which they discussed Flowcal. In a country obsessed with beautiful, svelte, sensual bodies, Flowcal was a sensation. The first month it was available, Brazilians flocked to drugstores and bought 300,000 boxes. Flowcal was so popular because seemed to offer the incredible possibility of losing weight not by *not* eating but, instead, *by* eating.

"You eat normally, but you get thinner," Thelma gushed. Flowcal, according to these women and many others, was a miracle.

"I've heard that the more fat you eat, the stronger the effect," Thaïs's friend Debora told her. Debora's seventy-year-old mother reacted like everyone else.

"Could it really be possible to lose weight without going on a diet?" she asked, clasping her hands as if in prayer. "That is truly a miracle!"

A miracle indeed. Based on our own personal conviction that something that sounds too good to be true is, more often than not, too good to be true, we remain skeptical in the face of claims like those of Thelma, Maria, and Debora. But we are anthropologists, not nutritionists or chemists. We are far from qualified to judge the veracity of the claims made for Flowcal in the mass media, and by many of the women we knew.

What interests us more than the truthfulness of the claims is the fact that the women believed them at all, especially with such conviction and gusto. Why were women like Thelma and Maria in such a frenzy about a diet product?

First World or Third World?

Anthropology teaches us that while a person's desires may feel intensely personal, they are shaped by the culture in which that person lives. It may seem a far-fetched claim initially, but Thelma and Maria's enthusiasm for the alleged transformative effects of Flowcal has to do with the fact that they live in a country wracked by a profound identity crisis.

Brazil has the tenth largest economy in the world and is one of the richest countries on earth. But it is a rich country full of poor people. Brazil has the dubious distinction of having one of the most unequal distributions of wealth in the world: the richest 20 percent of the population earns twenty-nine times as much as the poorest. Compare this to Mexico, where the richest 20 percent of the population earns sixteen times as much as the poorest, or the U.S., where the richest 20 percent of the population earns nine times as much as the poorest.[2]

In the U.S., where there are also sharp contrasts between the rich and the poor, nearly 70 percent of the population fall into the middle class, and about 20 percent are at the poverty line or below (usually defined as $1,400 a month for a family of four).[3] This means that the U.S. has an upper class that consists of about 10 percent of the population.

Brazil, too, has an upper class that consists of about 10 percent of the population. The difference is that the middle class accounts for only about 20 percent of the population. Seventy percent of the Brazilian population is poor, and roughly 30 percent of Brazilians live in abject poverty. That is, they earn less than $100 a month. Another 40 percent make less than $300 a month.[4]

These remarkable economic inequalities are linked to equally remarkable racial inequalities. Generally speaking, the whiter you are in Brazil, the richer you are. Of the poorest 10 percent of Brazilians, 60 percent are black or brown. Of the richest 10 percent, 83 percent are white. In education, nonwhites complete fewer years of study than whites. The average income of nonwhites is a little less than half that of whites. Afro-Brazilians have a life expectancy fourteen years shorter than that for whites, they have an infant mortality rate 30 percent higher, and they have more than double the proportion of illiterates.[5]

In addition to the prevalence of poverty and illiteracy throughout the country, Brazil's government, judiciary, and labor market are caught in a tension between old-style hierarchical thinking—

where you can acquire favors, rights, and privileges because of who you are and who you know—and individualistic, egalitarian ideals. It was only in 1989 that Brazil, for the first time in its history as an independent state, became a real democracy with free, fair, and competitive elections. The country's constitution asserts that Brazil is a modern, democratic country where all citizens should be treated equally. At the same time, however, the traditional, hierarchical heritage still persists in all kinds of contexts.[6]

This close coexistence of wealth and poverty, hierarchy, and egalitarianism has put many Brazilians in a quandary. Is their country a First World country—that is, is Brazil rich, advanced, modern, and white? Or is it a Third World country—that is, backward, dirty, poor, and of color? There are a lot of jokes in Brazil about the country's flag, which, in a way, symbolically embodies the problem. In the middle of the flag are printed the proud words "Order and Progress." Most Brazilians see those words as a hope or, more cynically, as a cruel taunt, rather than as a description of the way the country is organized or governed.

This quandary about whether Brazil is "really" a First World or a Third World country is particularly perplexing and pressing for people of the middle class, precisely because they are in the middle. They aren't rich, so they can't take for granted the power and privileges that automatically come with wealth. But they aren't poor, either—and they certainly don't want to be. But the extreme instability of the Brazilian economy (the country has changed and devalued its currency six times in the past twenty years[7]) makes their position a tense and fragile one. And they know it.

The way that people in Brazil, particularly people in the middle class, cope with this situation is to live their lives as though they personally are First World citizens, even if people around them are not. They do this by buying things that come from the First World, or encourage associations with it (cars, clothes, electronic devices, computers), traveling to the First World (charter trips to Europe and to the United States, where Disney World in Florida is the preferred destination), and thinking about and manipulating their bodies in ways that make them seem rich, advanced, and white.

Making Bodies

Nowhere in the world is the cult of the body beautiful as developed as it is in Brazil. Brazil has more plastic surgeons per capita than anywhere else in the world.[8] In 2001 there were 350,000 cosmetic surgery operations in a population of 170 million.[9] This is an impressive number for a nation where 60 percent of the working population earns less than 150 U.S. dollars per month.[10]

The general attitude in Brazil toward cosmetic surgery borders on reverence. Expressions such as "the power of scalpels," "the magic of cosmetic surgeries," and the "march toward scientific progress" are seen and heard everywhere. Brazil's most famous plastic surgeon, Ivo Pitanguy—whose claim to fame is a buttock lift that has been copied worldwide—is a household name. There are several glossy lifestyle magazines devoted to cosmetic surgery, with names like *Plastic Surgery and Beauty* and *Body and Plastic Surgery*. These sell almost as many copies per month as *Playboy*—which, by the way, is one of Brazil's biggest selling magazines.[11] One recurring *Playboy* cover girl, a dancer named Carla Perez, won a discount from her surgeon because she was a great advertisement for his work. She took advantage of the discount to pay for breast implants for her mother, sister, and sister-in-law.[12]

Brazil's contestant to the 2001 Miss Universe Pageant, twenty-two-year-old Juliana Borges, scandalized many non-Brazilians by speaking freely and frequently about the number and kinds of plastic surgeries she had undergone. These included breast implants, bioplastic sculpting in her cheekbones, silicone remolding in her chin, a sharpened jaw, pinned-back ears, and liposuction in her waistline and back.

"The same way someone has to study to become a doctor," Borges told reporters, "someone has to train. I have to work on my figure to get it where I want it . . . It's something I needed for my profession, for my work. I have a doctorate in body measurements."[13]

An eighteen-year-old middle-class girl named Claudia, whom Thaïs knew, subscribed to the same philosophy. After months of pleading, she finally convinced her parents to pay for breast reduction surgery. Claudia told Thaïs that she had several reasons for wanting this surgery: her breasts were too big, they were too heavy, and she could not wear T-shirts or dresses without using a bra.

"*Frente-unicas* [a kind of bodice that leaves the back bare] were in fashion and I was completely out of it. I couldn't wear anything!" Claudia said, exasperated. Now that she had managed to convince her parents to pay for the operation—in twelve monthly installments—she felt as though one of her dreams had come true. "I think I will be another person after this surgery!" she said.

Claudia was not the only one to anticipate the surgery with

excitement. One week before the procedure, her mother provided Thaïs with details.

"They've booked it for 7:30 A.M.," her mother explained. "But we have to be there one hour before that. The doctor said it will take about three hours, because first they do one breast and then the other. She will receive a general anesthesia, because it's a complicated procedure. They do the nipple first: I think they cut it and then they sew it. They build the whole breast anew. The doctor said that Claudia had so many glands. Too many glands. They'll have to go."

From an American or European perspective, the willingness with which people like Claudia and her mother talk about plastic surgery may seem surprising. Whereas cosmetic surgery in the U.S. or Europe is still seen as a private matter, and one that is slightly embarrassing or at least socially awkward, in Brazil surgeries like Claudia's are very public matters. Not only did everyone in Claudia's family know about her surgery, all her friends and colleagues did too.

Thaïs mentioned this to a mutual friend, Joana, who had introduced her to Claudia. Joana offered an interesting explanation.

"This procedure means one thing to them," Joana told Thaïs. "Status. To have plastic surgery is to show that you have the money to afford it. It's chic to talk about it. That's why Claudia and her family are talking so openly about it. It shows that they have money."

Indeed, some weeks later Thaïs heard a conversation between Joana and Claudia's mother. They were talking about the Italian porn star Cicciolina, who was playing a minor nonspeaking role in a popular *telenovela* that was being broadcast at the time. Inevitably, the subject of pornographic films arose.

Claudia's mother was perplexed. "I don't understand those films," she declared. "The women have enormous breasts. It's ugly! Those huge breasts bouncing. It must be because they don't have the money to pay for surgery."

Don has worked for several years among Brazilian transgendered prostitutes (called *travestis* in Portuguese).[4] For the past decade or so, a large number of those travestis have smuggled themselves into Italy to work the streets there, in hope of making much more money than they could ever dream of earning in Brazil, where their clients are generally much poorer. Sooner or later in Italy, one of several body modifications that most travestis undergo is a rhinoplasty to make their noses look tiny and pert. They do this because they find a straight, pointy little nose aesthetically more appealing than the broader Brazilian noses that most of them were born with. Travestis half-jokingly call these noses "LaToya Jackson noses." LaToya Jackson noses look fine on some travestis, but if you are a six-foot-tall Brazilian man with a head the size of a Halloween pumpkin, a tiny sylph of a nose looks decidedly odd.

Don mentioned this once to his travesti collaborator. He told her he felt sorry for travestis who paid so much money for nose jobs, only to end up with results looking so unnatural. Don's travesti friend looked at him in astonishment and laughed out loud. "You really don't understand anything, do you?" she said, shaking her head. "Of course they look unnatural. *That's the whole point.* How would anyone know that they had the money to pay for them if you couldn't tell the difference between what's natural and what has been bought?"

White Bodies

In Brazil, modifying one's body through surgery is about more than just becoming more beautiful and desirable. It is even about more than showing that you care about yourself, which is a phrase that frequently crops up whenever cosmetic surgery is discussed in the Brazilian mass media. (For example, Juliana Borges—Miss Brazil—explained that "I'm happy to show that any woman, even if she doesn't feel very pretty or very perfect, can make the effort to do this and fulfill a dream she would like to realize. I think this is now within reach."[5])

Instead, modifying your body in Brazil is fundamentally about displaying your wealth. But since money is associated with race (a well-known Brazilian proverb is *"O dinheiro embranquece"*— "Money whitens"), changing one's body is also about approximating whiteness.

Brazil is a country born out of a mixture of native peoples, Portuguese colonists, and African slaves. Slave traders shipped about four million slaves across the Atlantic to Brazil between the mid–sixteenth century to the mid–nineteenth century. This was more than one-third of all slaves transported across the Atlantic. (Compare this figure of four million to the figure of 661,000, which is the approximate number of slaves brought to the United States.[6])

What the slaves who were brought to Brazil encountered was a country with a tiny population of colonists—mostly men—and some indigenous people, many of whom were also slaves. The scarcity of white women, and the fact that white male colonialists could do what they wanted with their slaves, meant that very quickly a racially mixed population developed, with people who ranged across the color spectrum from black to white with complex gradations in between.

This mixture has always troubled the white elite. It became especially worrisome at the turn of the last century, after Brazil finally abolished slavery (the last country in the Western Hemisphere to do so) in 1888. At that point the Brazilian elite despaired over the enormous numbers of black people in the country. They believed that racial mixture had condemned Brazil to eternal backwardness and hopelessness.

Two related solutions to this problem were found. The first was to encourage, through various campaigns, more white people to emigrate to Brazil from Europe. From the late 1800s onward, the immigration of white people from Italy, Spain, Portugal, Poland, and Germany increased exponentially.

The second solution was the development of a policy of "whitening" the population. This basic idea here was that racial mixing, at the end of the day, wasn't perhaps such a bad thing after all. Miscegenation was not harmful to Brazil: on the contrary, the mixture of races ultimately benefited the Portuguese settlers. It made their mixed-race descendants better able to survive and thrive in the tropical Brazilian climate. Now, though, it was said, the dark past was over and the future belonged to those who were the whitest, partly because it was believed that white genes were stronger in the long run, and partly because people "naturally" wanted partners with lighter skin, since whiter skin was considered more attractive and desirable.

Although the grosser forms of this kind of racist thinking are no longer widely espoused in Brazil, the fact that race is not so much an either/or matter—as it is in the United States, where you are either black *or* white—means that individuals, to a certain extent, can assert their own racial affiliation on a broad racial continuum. But the fact that whiteness remains connected to wealth, power, and privilege also means that most people opt *up* the racial ladder toward whiteness, rather than down, toward blackness. It is something of a joke in Brazil that there are about 160 euphemisms one can choose from to avoid having to utter the words "I am black."

"Everything Is Tastier with No-Cal"

What has all this got to do with diet products like Flowcal? Let us explain this by looking closely at a television commercial for another diet product. The product being advertised here is No-Cal, a sugar substitute. The commercial features two well-known actresses and a popular actor. The women are in their thirties, and they are famous primarily for always playing rich, desirable characters in *telenovelas*. The man is in his late forties or early fifties, dignified, stately, and also known for always playing rich, desirable characters in *telenovelas*. All three are white. They have pale, light complexions and straight, dark hair.

The commercial opens with a mid-shot of Carolina Ferraz, one of the actresses. She is sitting leisurely in a dining chair, in front of a table covered with a white cloth. The whole setting is very white and bright. Behind her one sees a huge window and a green, unfocused background. This could be a restaurant, a spa, or even Carolina Ferraz's private home. She is wearing a white cardigan, her hair is tied in a ponytail, and her only adornment is a small pair of discreet, expensive-looking earrings. She is holding a cup of ice cream in one hand and a spoon in the other. She looks at the camera and says, "You are probably wondering: how come Carolina is so thin, when she eats this much?"

The shot cuts to the other actress, Silvia Pfeiffer. She is also sitting in a chair in front of a white table. The background is also unfocused, very light and bright. It suggests the atmosphere of an expensive restaurant. Silvia Pfeiffer has short hair, pearl earrings, and a white dress or top that leaves her shoulders visible. She is filmed in a mid-shot, from the waist up. Looking placidly at the camera, she answers Carolina's question: "She uses No-Cal!"

We cut back to Carolina Ferraz and the same setting as in the first shot. "With No-Cal"—Carolina smiles—"I take away the calories of my juice, of my coffee, of my dessert."

Now the scene changes to a mid-shot of José Mayer, the actor. He is standing, wearing a white T-shirt and an open white shirt. He faces the camera. "Isn't it nice," he asks, "to cut calories but still eat tasty food?" He raises a little cup of coffee—which is also white—as if toasting the camera, takes a sip, and winks.

Silvia Pfeiffer, in close-up: "Do you want advice? No-Cal has almost *no* calories."

José Mayer, in extreme close-up: "You don't need to get rid of taste in order to get rid of calories."

Silvia Pfeiffer, in extreme close-up: "And besides that, with No-Cal, your coffee tastes much better."

Carolina Ferraz, in close-up: "Everything," she says suggestively, "is tastier with No-Cal."

Carolina smiles at the camera, and the forty-second commercial ends.[7]

In a way, this commercial is no different from hundreds of others broadcast around the globe, trying to tempt people into using products that they are probably better off without. But there is more to this commercial than the hawking of a sugar substitute. A specific *Brazilian* message is being conveyed here, one that highlights all of the concerns we have been discussing so far, including First Worldness, wealth, and whiteness.

The first thing to notice is that everything in the commercial is white: the clothes, the decor, the people, even the cup from which José Mayer sips coffee. Whiteness like this is a very common way in Brazil of representing wealth. In *telenovelas*, those mainstays of Brazilian television, for example, it is very common to see living rooms of the upper and upper middle classes furnished with predominantly white, somewhat futuristic furniture that gives the rooms a light and bright atmosphere.

There is also an economy to this aesthetic of using whiteness to represent privileged milieus. White furniture, settings, and clothes require more work to be kept clean. Having a white living room implies that one also has the money to afford people (usually nonwhite maids, washers, and cleaners) to keep the white white.

Another connection between whiteness, wealth, and the First World is the association one might make between whiteness and hospitals, clinics, and doctors. A commercial like this, filmed entirely in a white ambience, encourages viewers to associate No-Cal with science, advanced technology, and First World know-how.

Of course, diet products like No-Cal and the very idea of going on a diet in the first place are, in themselves, associated with wealth. A sugar substitute such as the one in this commercial costs much more than sugar. The commercial is structured around the idea that *you*—provided that *you* have the money—will be able to sip *your* artificially sweetened coffee, drink *your* juice, and eat *your* dessert without gaining any weight. But in a country like Brazil, where experts estimate that thirty-two million people—that is, one in five Brazilians—go hungry every day, this kind of preoccupation to avoid calories is, to put it mildly, a class-specific concern.

Leaking Out the Third World

All of which brings us back at last to Flowcal. A few days before the national celebration of Carnival—the time of the year when Brazilians of all ages, colors, and classes get down and shake their purposefully scantily clad bodies for up to a whole week—Thelma, who wanted to be ready, finally managed to purchase a box of Flowcal and start taking it. She and her friend Maria told Thaïs in gory detail how the diet pill worked.

Thelma, Maria shrieked with excitement, was "leaking fat"!

"We were sitting in Thelma's living room, talking about life," Maria said. "Then the phone rang and Thelma got up to answer it. That's when I saw that her pants and the sofa where she was sitting were stained with something that looked like oil. Thelma didn't even notice it! She was leaking fat and she couldn't help it."

Thelma, who was thrilled, continued Maria's description.

"And I remember that that day my stomach was almost empty. But the more fat food you eat, the stronger the effect. Fat food can give you diarrhea. If you eat something fat, then you have to be prepared and stay at home! And when you go to the bathroom, if you look, it looks just like when you pour oil into water. You can actually see little lumps of dissolved fat!"

The ironic thing is that what Thelma and Maria described may in fact have been a side effect of Flowcal, not a sign of its efficacy. The patient information leaflet that comes with the pills lists common side effects: "oily spotting, gas with discharge, urgent need to go to the bathroom, oily or fatty stools, an oily discharge, increased number of bowel movements, and inability to control bowel movements."

No matter, though. The two friends were clearly not interested in the fine print. They wanted results and they got them, even if it meant a stained sofa and oily trousers.

The results they wanted were not just the loss of fat: what they wanted to lose by taking Flowcal and beginning to literally leak was any connection to the Third World, poverty, and people of color. They wanted all of that expelled from their bodies and flushed away from their sight.

Flowcal is talked about as a modern drug and a miraculous cure for misplaced fat. Like other cutting-edge diet products, Flowcal originates in the First World, in this case from a laboratory in Switzerland—a country that many Brazilians consider to be the epitome of a developed and wealthy First World nation. An aura of scientific complexity and modernity emanates from products like Flowcal, and they are presented in advertisements and everyday conversations as having an almost magical power. And indeed their true effects are more magical than real. By spending more than most of their fellow countrymen earn in month for a box of diet pills that give them diarrhea and oily discharges, women like Thelma and Maria can luxuriate in the fantasy that they live lives similar to the rich Brazilian women in cities who keep getting thinner as the rest of the globe gets fatter. Flowcal puts them in touch with Carolina Ferraz and Silvia Pfeiffer. It makes them attractive for José Mayer. When they swallow a Flowcal, Thelma and Maria are swallowing particular Brazilian fantasies of class, race, order, and progress. Flowcal is the whole First World in a little blue pill.

Lard

Jillian R. Cavanaugh

On a balmy summer evening a few years ago, I had dinner with a friend at Tre Torri, "Three Towers," a rustic restaurant in the oldest neighborhood in Bergamo, Italy. Tre Torri prides itself on serving traditional Bergamasco food. When the appetizer arrived, the waitress exclaimed: *"Lo provi, signorina! È delizioso!"* (Try it, you'll like it!) She smiled mischieviously. Was it a dare or encouragement? I wasn't sure. I looked down at my plate to find snow-white curls, moist and slightly shiny, looking like slimy little pieces of squid. The curls were carefully rolled up, flush up against small pieces of toast.

"Con pepe, si mangia," the waitress said, *"un po' di pepe e basta!"* She wanted me to eat it with pepper.

Never one to back down in the face of a challenge, especially not a culinary one, I speared a curl of the white stuff with my fork and put it in my mouth. It melted. It wasn't fishy, nor was it even slimy. Instead it was delicate and light, if a bit greasy. Hardly surprising, though, since what I had in my mouth was *lardo*.

Lardo is white pig fat that has been cured and thinly sliced, to be sure, but still . . . it's white pig fat all the same. In fancy Italian restaurants in the United States, high-end chefs will often disguise *lardo* by naming it "white prosciutto." The truth, though, is that *lardo* is not prosciutto, white or otherwise. *Lardo* is lard.

Today, lard is regarded as a delicacy in Bergamo, as it is across the rest of Italy. It is a local treasure from the past that people regard as an appetizing start to many a rich meal. In expensive restaurants, I have seen numerous stylishly dressed people tuck into a plate of lard with sincere gusto.

But lard has not always been treated as a rarefied specialty. Consider the recipe from a Bergamasco cookbook for *minèstra di lard*—lard soup. Lard soup is easy to make and calls for only a few ingredients: local lard, a garlic clove, half a cabbage, rice, salt, pepper, and some *grana* or hard cheese like Parmesan. It is substantial and nourishing, and would have constituted a meal in and of itself. But in this heavy peasant form, lard soup is really the antithesis of the thin slivers of lard-as-delicacy appetizer that I encountered at the Tre Torri restaurant. Restaurants like the Tre Torri purport to serve genuine Bergamasco fare, but they rarely offer dishes like lard soup. Instead they provide modern renderings of traditional foods. These modern renderings suggest the past, but they refine it into thin, appetizing slices of flavor.

. . .

Bergamascos—the name for the people who live in Bergamo—are not the only ones to repackage their comfort foods, of course. Just think of the recent wave of restaurants serving new versions of American comfort foods like gourmet macaroni and cheese, designer mashed potatoes, and spruced-up BLTs. Why does this sort of thing happen? And why does it seem that fatty foods, in particular, often play a starring role in such transformations of homey, old-fashioned local foods into delicacies?

These are not trivial questions. On the contrary, processes such as these are intertwined with social, economic, and political histories. Bergamascos' continued—though transformed—attachment to lard illuminates how intimate, personal elements of everyday life like food preferences are connected to larger social and economic trends such as rapid transformation from a peasant society to one that is industrialized. In many ways the story of lard is an allegory of the modernization of Bergamo, reflecting how the town itself has changed since the Second World War. As a culinary object undergoing transformation from peasant staple to elite treat, lard, in an odd way, is a symbol of Bergamo itself.

Lying to the northeast of Italy's fashion capital, Milan, Bergamo is off the beaten track for American tourists. In contrast to the rural towns in Tuscany or Umbria, which sit atop picturesque hills adorned by vineyards and olive groves, Bergamo is hemmed in by an industrial wasteland. Myriad businesses, large and small, line the fifteen miles of autostrada from Milan to Bergamo. These freeways and industries attest to a greater material wealth than can be found in those Tuscan hill towns, even if the view is less charming. Nonetheless, Bergamo has a rich, distinctive local history, and Bergamascos express deep-seated attachments to their cultural heritage. As I saw at the Tre Torri that night, one of the ways they express this attachment is by eating fat—unadorned, pure fat.

Modernity and Tradition

Becoming modern—a situation characterized by industrialization, technological advancement, and "social progress"—in Bergamo, as in all parts of Italy, has gone hand in hand with becoming "more Italian." This may sound strange, for Bergamo—like Rome, Venice, and the hill towns of Tuscany—now seems to be naturally a part of Italy. However, the modern nation of Italy has existed only for a little more than one hundred years. Before the 1860s, Italy was divided into city-states and individually governed provinces, all of which had their own particular identities, distinctive dialects, and beloved local cuisines.

The issue of how "Italian" Italians feel themselves to be—as opposed to feeling, say, Sicilian or Florentine—has been problematic for the national government throughout the twentieth century. For instance, only 2 percent of the country's population spoke Italian when Italy was united in the 1860s. People spoke local dialects, which are really quite different languages, even if they are related. At the time of Italy's unification, the only people who actually knew Italian were the educated elite classes. These percentages did not begin to shift substantially until the 1950s and 1960s, when access to universalized education, the emergence of national Italian language television, radio, and newspapers and magazines, and the increasing advantage to speaking Italian in the workplace began to affect what language parents chose to speak with their children.

At the same time that Italians began to speak Italian and started to think of themselves as Italians—and not just Romans or Venetians, for instance—Italy, and particularly northern Italy, was experiencing an economic boom. Before the Second World War, Italy was mostly a rural society dependent on agriculture. This was especially true in Bergamo, once a poor province where people sometimes had to turn to chestnuts (notoriously poor in nutrition) as a staple food during the hungry winter months. Since the 1950s, however, Italian cities and towns have grown; the people have benefited from the economic opportunities of industrialization and, more recently, a shift into a postindustrial service economy. Most of the material deprivations of Bergamo's past have been left behind. But many of the objects emblematic of their past impoverished existence have suddenly experienced a renaissance among Bergamascos.

In times of rapid change, people often come to feel nostalgic about the past that they have lost. One way they express this nostalgia is through collecting artifacts from the past, from local tools and utensils to proverbs and nursery rhymes. Not surprisingly, the people of Bergamo are newly interested in connecting their contemporary everyday lives to the lives their ancestors lived in the past, and are doing so by reclaiming some of the things from these bygone days. What Bergamascos want to revive is the sense of shared community, identity, and history. They want to promote the idea of the past as a time when "we" all ate the same simple foods, spoke the same straightforward dialect, and embraced an ethic of hard work and honesty. Bergamascos are attempting, in other words, to reconcile their current ways of living—similar to how people live all over Italy and the rest of the modern, globalized world—with their humbler past and peasant traditions. This goal does not necessarily clash with the material prosperity that Bergamascos have earned over the last sixty years and are currently enjoying. But that doesn't mean that it is entirely unproblematic, either, as it is clear that only certain parts of the past are seen as desirable and worth saving. No one wants to return, for instance, to the days when there wasn't enough to eat, or when education was an elite privilege and children worked in the fields from an early age. Embracing and consuming symbolic objects—like lard—allows Bergamascos to be connected to what they see as the wealth of their past, not its poverty. And in this case, fat is more than a metaphor for the good life; it is a living symbol of community.

Consuming Culture

The taste or preference for certain foods are often closely linked to membership in particular groups. Southerners in the United States are said to be partial to grits; people from Maine are believed to love their lobster; and it is hard to think about Texas without thinking barbecue, or Wisconsin without thinking cheese. Of course, you can always find exceptions to these generalizations—there are certainly vegans in Texas and Wisconsin—but these foods are indelibly linked to people and place.

The sensory experience of taste is highly personal, but it is also culturally socialized. Think, for example, of how we on the one hand consider individual tastes for foods as being immutable ("I just don't like eggplant"), but how on the other hand we connect certain foods to particular cultural backgrounds

("The Germans like beer and bratwurst," or "The French like rich food"). From this perspective, it is easy to see that the experience of eating lard can become a way of identifying oneself as a distinctively Bergamasco person, as well as a way of tasting and experiencing Bergamasco traditions and collective identity.

But in order for a food like lard to play a role as a symbol of tradition, it has to appear to retain the same salient qualities across generations. There can be no such thing as "lite" lard or low-sodium lard. In other words, it has to look like the same creamy, porky substance that it always was; it has to taste and look "genuine."

Appearances do not tell the whole story, however. Today's lard, whatever the rhetoric to the contrary, is not exactly the same thing it has always been. The process of producing lard in Bergamo has greatly altered over the last several decades. Lard used to be made exclusively on a small scale, often for a family's private consumption. Butchers and grocers in town would have personal ties to farmers in the countryside, who raised and slaughtered their own pigs. Either the farmers or the butchers themselves carried out the intensive process of curing the pig to create lard and other cured pork products, such as prosciutto and pancetta.

Nowadays the Italian government and European Union (EU) seek to standardize and industrialize production of a number of small-scale, locally produced animal products such as cheeses or sausages. The production of lard has been affected too. For instance, EU legislators have tried to outlaw using marble surfaces while curing lard. They demand that stainless-steel surfaces be used instead, because they are easier to sterilize. But lard producers complain that it is the very porousness of the marble that gives the lard its distinctive flavor.[1] Many small-scale farmers today defy national and European laws like this by operating just under the radar of regulators, claiming to produce products for personal consumption while selling them under the table to friends.

Changing Tastes

In Italy, a number of regions are especially renowned for their cuisine, and are acknowledged as places where *"si mangia bene!"* (you eat well!). Bergamo, alas, is not one of those places. In contrast to the refined simplicity of Tuscan cooking, the bold combinations of ingredients that grace Roman cooking, or the Mediterranean intersection of flavors perfected over centuries in Sicily and Naples, Bergamasco cuisine is considered by other Italians to be rather bland. Although Bergamascos have integrated foods from other parts of the peninsula into their daily eating habits—they now eat pasta and pizza regularly, for example—they remain loyal to their culinary roots, often choosing local products over more prestigious goods from other regions.

Lard is a perfect example of this. *Lardo di Colonnata* from Tuscany is widely considered to be the best—and most expensive—lard, and is available in Bergamo.[2] But Bergamasco consumers often ask for local lard (*lardo nostrano*) in their local delis. Even the large chain supermarkets that have sprung up on the outskirts of Bergamo stock local lard, as well as the more famous varieties, because their customers ask for it, claiming that their traditional recipes just would not taste the same without it.

Local city administrators are doing what they can to support Bergamo's culinary traditions. Recently, Bergamo's Office of

Commerce, Industry, and Artisans started a local association called the Bergamo Città dei Mille . . . Sapori (City of the Thousand . . . Tastes). The name of this project plays on Bergamo's self-endowed nickname, the Città dei Mille (City of the Thousand), which derives from its historical role of sending a thousand troops to accompany Giuseppe Garibaldi on his mission to bring Sicily into the nascent Italian nation during the unification of Italy in the 1860s.

The City of the Thousand Tastes project picks out locally valued foods, such as lard, and promotes them as examples of "quality and tradition." This initiative may be a vital first step toward gaining the powerful DOC (Denominazione di Origine Controllata, or Denomination of Controlled Origin) label, which protects products and their production processes as identifiable with certain geographic regions. DOC is a nationally bestowed and internationally recognized marker of prestige, and it carries legal status. The DOC label is applied to food products and wine that are judged distinctive of a particular locality or region in Italy and produced according to traditional methods. This is similar to how "real" champagne can only be made in the Champagne region of France. (Sparkling wine made in other regions can be called "sparkling wine," but it is illegal to call it "champagne.") Consumers know that buying a DOC product means they are getting the real thing, and hence, they are willing to pay a higher price than for a non-DOC product, endowing DOC producers with both symbolic and material capital. The DOC label for Bergamasco lard may be perceived as an endorsement of Bergamascos' past and palate.

The City of a Thousand Tastes initiative, then, aims to preserve certain foods in their traditional forms. But at this point the question arises: with any number of foods to choose from—such as the eggs produced from local breeds of chickens, or the distinctive varieties of greens that grow wild in the mountains behind Bergamo—why did officials in Bergamo single out lard, with its enormous fat and cholesterol content, as one of Bergamo's representative thousand tastes?

It turns out that nearly all the foods supported by the city's initiative are fatty animal products: cured meats like lard, sausages, and a number of cheeses. Polenta, which for centuries has been a staple carbohydrate in the area, is the only exception. However, polenta is never eaten without some form of animal fat in accompaniment, two of the most popular being cheese or local sausages called *löanghina*. While polenta may make up the bulk of the meal, it is the fatty accompaniments that add necessary calories and the beloved and prized salty, fatty flavor. And when you look at the menus of restaurants in Bergamo that serve "authentic" Bergamasco food, fatty foods hold places of honor there as well. A few items appear on every menu: in addition to polenta and *casonsèi* (Bergamasco ravioli served with browned butter, pancetta, and crispy sautéed sage leaves), *salumi nostrani* (local cured meats, including lard) is one of them. Although polenta was the staple that kept many families alive during the lean years, authentic Bergamasco cooking these days accords higher prestige to the cured and roasted meats and other animal fats that were dense sources of essential calories and protein as well as flavor.

In fact, it may be that lard has been chosen precisely because of its fatty nature. Fat is flavor, after all. Many Americans decry the fat content of bacon, but Sizzlean, that low-fat turkey bacon substitute from the 1980s, never caught on. Consumers clearly wanted bacon's genuine porky—and fatty—flavor. Fatty foods, as culinary historians note, are often prized as specialties due to their satisfying taste. Think of French goose-liver pâté, English Stilton cheese, Buffalo chicken wings, or even Southern fried chicken—all extremely fatty foods that people identify as the specialties of particular places and value for their unique, rich tastes. Such foods can also convey a certain amount of social prestige: that's what sets them apart from the mundane everyday fat of a McDonald's cheeseburger. This social prestige is demonstrated by a number of factors: the restrictions placed on who the rightful producers of these foods are, the idea that there are "real" and "fake" versions of them, as well as the high price they usually command. And don't forget that many of these specialties require one to "acquire" preferences for them—something that can usually be achieved only by those who can afford it. Anthropologist Polly Weissner observes that these types of fatty foods, preferred for their taste, "are often associated with well-being and confer superiority on those who can regularly produce, consume or distribute them."[3] In certain parts of Europe, it is often pork products that have a particular cachet (think of all those types of Spanish ham), so perhaps it isn't too surprising that pig fat in Bergamo is saturated with symbolic weight.

But as I noted before, the lard eaten today is not the exactly the lard that was eaten in the past. Just look at how lard is displayed in the City of the Thousand Tastes literature. Slices of lard are attractively arranged on a platter, framed by loaves of bread and a glass of red wine. The lard is also pictured in a photograph with other local cured meats. Similarly, in restaurants lard can be ordered either on its own or as part of an assortment of cured meats, sometimes arranged according to color and fat content, with more lean meats like cured horse—yes, cured *horse*—on one side of the platter and lard as its pale white opposite on the other, with pancetta and other red and white marbled meats in between. Either way, lard stands out to be savored on its own merits, not as one ingredient among many, as it was in traditional dishes like lard soup. Now lard is brought onto center stage (or plate) as a soloist, a luxurious exemplar of Bergamasco cuisine and culture.

The taste of necessity, then, has been transformed into the taste of luxury and sophistication. Another perusal of the same cookbook that featured lard soup demonstrates that not all "traditional" foods are commonly savored in Bergamo's restaurants or promoted as one of the city's thousand tastes. One that stood out for me was *ciocolàt de sàngh*, which translates literally as "blood chocolate." Blood chocolate is cow's blood that is boiled until it becomes dense, hard, and a "good red-brown color," then cooled, sliced, and eaten like chocolate. This is not a dish that one runs into in Bergamo today with any regularity, which demonstrates that just because something is produced locally and was eaten in the past is not in itself sufficient reason for it to be cherished. Dishes must also appeal to modern Italian palates— palates that can luxuriate in lard without having to eat it as a primary source of nutrition.

Perhaps it is this dimension of prestige and luxury that provides the answer to our question, "Why save fatty foods?" Where once these fats were necessary, providing essential calories while adding flavor, modern eaters don't need those fat calories in their diets. And precisely for that reason, they can afford to desire them. In addition, in just the same way that I might justify ordering a fat-laden dish of "homemade" macaroni and cheese because it's so "homey" (even when the macaroni and cheese only comes out of a box), Bergamascos look at their *lardo* and find "home." In the slimy white slices of fat, they find all that is good about their culture. The cream of their culture, one might say, has risen to the top, been skimmed off, and fashioned into a forkful—or perhaps whole plate—of delicious, nostalgic fat.

Indulgence

Margaret Willson

The scene is a chic coffee café in urban Seattle. The barista flicks his towel over a spotless wooden counter.

"What would you like?" he asks the woman standing before him. She is wearing a short black leather jacket and jeans.

"A tall mocha, please."

"Will that be with whole, two percent, or skim?"

"Hmmm, you'd better make that skim." The woman glances at her female companion, whose hair is cut in a perfect pageboy. "That won't make it taste too much like water, will it?" Her companion smiles and nods an acknowledgment of her friend's self-control. "I really like skim better than two percent anyway. It tastes better."

"Would you like whipped cream on that?" the barista asks.

"Oh." The woman looks into her billfold as if to find an answer lurking there. "Well, that would taste really good, wouldn't it?"

The barista smiles.

"Sure," the woman says. "I deserve it." She looks at the barista and then looks away. He spritzes on the whipped cream. The woman turns to her friend and says, "We deserve these sinful indulgences, don't we?"

Her friend gives a quick tight smile. "Yes, of course." She turns to the barista. "I'll have a double Americano." She pauses. "And I'll take that last cinnamon roll too. But put the butter on the side, would you?"

I have seen variations of this scene enacted time after time in coffee cafés, where I often sit with my laptop, ostensibly working. I am always intrigued by the obvious contradiction that gets played out again and again in these cafés: the apparent mixture of indulgence and restraint in this particular type of consumption. Most customers order a skimmed-milk drink—and add whipped cream. Or they order a low-fat pastry—with butter or frosting on the side. I do it myself: if I allow myself my favorite apricot and walnut scone, I take 2 percent milk in my coffee. If I skip the scone, I get half-and-half (lots of it, actually).

Why bother with the pretense? I asked myself one day as I sipped my creamy coffee and watched five other people make the same kinds complicated decisions I had just made. Do we think that the skim milk somehow cancels out the whipped cream?

These observations, and occasional conversations with Eric,

one of my favorite baristas, eventually got me curious about the way Americans consume fat in public places. I live in Seattle, and I know that we Seattleites like to imagine ourselves as outdoorsy and healthy. Hiking and skiing and kayaking play a central role in how we identify ourselves as Northwesterners. We spend time, and a lot of money, on the gear-clad appearance of good health. But if we really cared about good health, it seems to me that everyone would skip the mocha or cream and just drink plain black coffee. Or, better yet, green tea. But that was not what I saw happening. Instead, what I saw happening in coffee cafés is that people order fat-free milk and fatty cream in the very same drink. Why?

In asking this question, I immediately encountered all sorts of surprising tensions between indulgence, morality, pleasure, and restraint. This struggle to find balance between all these things is not a purely American dilemma, to be sure. But there does exist a particularly American way of negotiating the line between indulgence and restraint. How and why those negotiations look like they do began to intrigue me.

The Rise of the Coffee Café

According to the Specialty Coffee Association of America, Americans drink more than three million cups of coffee daily. Sixty-six percent of these are drunk away from home. Seattle boasts over 650 coffee cafés, including 318 of that "fast-food" dynamo of coffee cafés, Starbucks. An estimated two hundred thousand espresso shots are served here daily.[1]

Espresso consumption is considered so vital to Seattle public life and its economy that a recent initiative proposed to the

City of Seattle to place a ten-cent "luxury" tax on espresso drinks caused an uproar. This tax was going to subsidize programs for early-childhood learning, and it only targeted drinks made with espresso, such as lattes and mochas. Good old American filtered drip coffee was exempt. But even though the tax was earmarked for an undeniably admirable cause, the Seattle City Council was so distressed by this assault on Seattle's hallmark drink that it delayed the vote on the initiative eight months. Two hundred protesters of the initiative staged a Seattle version of the 1773 Boston Tea Party, and coffee café owners threw burlap bags, designed to resemble coffee sacks, into the waters of a local urban lake, in a sure move to attract attention from coffee-drinking dog walkers and joggers.

In the end, Seattle voters roundly defeated the initiative. The result of the vote was reported in a local newspaper under the banner headline of LATTE TAX CREAMED.[2]

What is it about a product like coffee that makes it so sacrosanct?

Perhaps it has something to do with the fact that coffee has increasingly become something that Americans consume in public, in particular kinds of places. Those places, coffee cafés, are designed to be special kinds of public places. The decor, the ambience, the special language known only to the cognoscenti—"A venti decaf hazelnut latte, 2 percent"—all of this is supposed to make you feel sophisticated, worldly, in touch with the urbane. Coffee cafés are geared toward a yuppie crowd, with some residual influence from older "bohemian" coffeehouses that have existed since the 1960s.

The rise of these new coffee cafés, and of "gourmet" specialty coffee more generally, is the result of marketing genius. In the early 1960s the corporate giants General Foods, Nestlé, and Procter & Gamble dominated the coffee market. Only four roasters controlled 75 percent of the trade. Coffee mostly came instant or from cans. Throughout the 1960s, coffee-drinking among people under fifty began to decline. Anthropologist William Roseberry writes that the coffee marketers of the time were concerned that this decline was attributed to the fact that younger people associated coffee with an elderly lifestyle they wanted to reject. By the 1980s the situation looked dire for coffee marketers, who saw their market aging and dying off.[3]

Sharp-minded entrepreneurs in the late 1980s and early 1990s began gearing specific coffee products to the emerging young professional market. These new entrepreneurs began promoting coffees with a marketing campaigns that were affiliated with social justice groups such as Equal Exchange ("a Fair Trade company distributing Organic and Fair Trade products in the independent natural food sector") and Coffee Kids ("an international nonprofit organization established to improve the quality of life for children and families who live in coffee-growing communities around the world"). The ties to social causes did not, however, prevent the new coffee companies from making significant profits: the markup from the wholesale green beans to the coffee café retail price was between 400 and 600 percent. Coffee was also marketed as if it came from exotic locales. The clever and purposely misleading use of the word *style* also came into play during this time; so instead of Kenyan or Brazilian coffee, what we got was "Kenyan style," made of beans that were grown nowhere near Africa, let alone Kenya.

Along with new coffee "styles" came "flavored" coffee—that is, coffee infused with natural or artificial flavorings that make the beverage taste as un-coffeelike as possible. This had the advantage of appealing to younger consumers who might otherwise have selected a soft drink. The invention of flavored coffees extended the market to reach even those people who do not particularly like coffee but who want a jolt or who want to be part of the current scene.[4]

Throughout the 1990s, specialty coffee cafés, from Starbucks to small privately owned enterprises, multiplied in every middle-class and commercial neighborhood in the U.S. More recently, coffee cafés have even begun to pop up in the more economically challenged neighborhoods, such as the predominately African American neighborhood where I live. The opening of the first Starbucks in this area caused dispute because most locals knew that the space, a prime location, had been in negotiation for some two years by a popular local restaurant specializing in catfish. City and local authorities, however, inclined toward the Starbucks, presumably because they thought it would bring in outside business and cast a more middle-class glow over the area.

And if that indeed was their intention, they were right. The Starbucks that opened has been careful to make itself a "cool," jazzy, and middle-class place with an African American "style." It has become one of the few places in the neighborhood where whites and blacks appear to feel comfortable to sit together in the same place, socializing if they wish and, for the price of a fairly expensive cup of coffee, looking like yuppies regardless of the actual state of their personal finances.

Throughout America, in any city, we can all see the success of the modern coffee café. But what about our choices once we get there? What about our mochas, Frappuccinos, and lattes? Why, exactly, are we so drawn to these places, and what they offer?

Fat and Fat Lite

Few things in society are as imbued with as much meaning as are sex and eating. Coffee cafés do their best to subtly link the two. A photo ad in one Seattle coffee café I frequent shows a young, well-built man in his tight T-shirt, licking frothy curls from the top of his latte. Other ads show creamy froth in richly textured detail that give it a sensually inviting look. Feminist writer Rosalind Coward has called ads like this "food pornography." She argues that they appeal to our secret desire for the forbidden.[5]

Starbucks, according to some health watchdogs, are food pornographers in more ways than one. Two new products, the Strawberries & Crème Frappuccino Blended Crème and the Double Chocolate Chip Frappuccino Blended Crème recently earned the "Food Porn of the Month Award" from the Center for the Science in the Public Interest's (CPSI) Nutrition Action Healthletter.[6] Past winners of the award include the Coconut Crème Frappuccino and the Vanilla Crème Frappuccino.[7] This award is not for the best hard-core food ad but for food products the CPSI considers to be impressively unhealthy. A 20-ounce venti of either of these products has over 600 calories and while the Strawberries & Crème has 7 grams of fat, the Double Chocolate Chip Frappuccino contains 16 grams of fat.[8,9] (Venti means "really big" for those not fluent in American coffee café Italian). Neither drink actually contains coffee; the Nutrition Action Healthletter calls them "fattuccinos"—more like milk shakes than coffee.[10]

Starbucks did not become the commercial giant it is by accident. As one slim man I interviewed said, "I figure I'm not drinking cream for my health. It's for comfort." Even more revealingly, a young woman told me, "The fat doesn't really count if it's a drink."

Starbucks and other coffee café drink designers understand a fundamental principle: Americans love fat. They love the way it tastes and looks. In fact, the American diet derives 60 percent of its calories from two nutrients: sugar and fat. The average American eats 135 pounds of fat per year. This translates to *one ton* every fifteen years."

There is a lot of talk these days about how the American love of fat is new. But if tradition and history mean anything, it isn't, really. Americans have always had a "fat tooth." The food historian Richard Hooker writes that in the 1700s, butter and oils flavored the dishes of all classes in colonial America. Melted butter, served in a cup or boat, was routinely served with both meats and vegetables. Hooker cites the journal of an early traveler to America who concluded that the only American sauce, even for roast beef, was melted butter. Americans' "turnips and potatoes swim in hog's lard, butter or fat." Pork fat routinely flavored baked beans, chowder, porridge, vegetables, and even puddings and pies. On the frontier, bear's oil and venison grease served the same purpose. Because of this obsession with the taste of fat, some Europeans reportedly called the Americans "Buttermouths."[12]

Despite this history, and despite our current reality of impressive fat consumption, Americans of today are obsessed with appearing as though we are avoiding fat. It is intriguing to note that the kind of fat Americans are eating is changing. The Institute of Shortening and Edible Oils divides fats into two major categories: "visible" and "invisible" fats. What the institute calls invisible fats are those contained in milk or meats. Visible or "added" fats are fats we add to other foods: products like salad dressings, spreads and processed foods. In the period from 1970 to 1997, the consumption of invisible fat decreased but the eating of visible fat climbed—yet the eating of visible fat seemed clandestine.[3] When I discovered this statistic, I reflected back on the people in the coffee cafés, dripping skim milk (invisible fat) into their drink and then spraying on the whipped cream (visible fat), taking the fat out of the milk and then adding it back (and then some) to improve the taste.

Americans' preoccupation with slimness while we are, at the same time, growing ever fatter presents an intriguing anomaly. "Lite" and diet foods remain overwhelming popular despite the introduction of diets that actually encourage fat consumption, such as the Atkins diet. Total fat intake had a short-lived decline in 1994 with the introduction in supermarkets of mandatory nutrition labeling. Food companies also introduced over five thousand lower fat versions of food between 1995 and 1997.[4] According to the American Obesity Association, consumers now spend about $30 billion per year on weight-loss-related products. Yet, overall total food consumption has dramatically increased over the last thirty years. For women, half of whom are supposedly on a diet at any one given time, the increase is three times as much as for men, with women's food intake increasing 22 percent to men's 7 percent increase. More revealing, in relation to us café coffee consumers, is the fact that the decline in total fat intake after the introduction of low-fat foods was so short-lived, in part because people decided they did not like the taste of the low-fat or no-fat products. So they either returned to the full-fat version or else they added fat to their supposedly low-fat item to improve the taste. Although the total consumption of milk went down between 1970 and 2000, the consumption of both skim milk and half and half went up, skim by 150 percent and half-and-half by 47 percent.[5]

As anthropologist Sidney Mintz has observed, the consumption of fat and the consumption of low-fat anything are increasing simultaneously. In other words, what is happening is that Americans are eating more fats and sugar, yet at the same time they are buying other, low-fat foods to make them feel less guilty. And they are eating *those* too.[6]

Immoral Fat

Think of the triple-scoop ice-cream cone, the pie à la mode, the bonbon. Foods like these don't represent sustenance; they represent indulgence, a gift. They conjure up images of rapture, bliss. Our lattes and mochas are anything but sustenance; we want them because they make us feel happy. We also know they are not very good for us. Our small indiscretions are all the more exciting because they represent a kind of danger, harbingers of our potential falls from grace and self-control. Each of us thinks we are making our own individual choices here, and of course we are. But we are also responding to moral messages that have been honed over several generations.

The connections between denial and indulgence in America find an early example during Prohibition. The closure of saloons during Prohibition led to the booming popularity of the ice-cream parlor. From today's perspective, what could be more innocent and wholesome than ice cream? At the time, though, the idea of men and women sitting together, chatting and laughing as they spooned luscious, fat-filled ice cream into their mouths was too much for many of the keepers of the public morality. Ice-cream parlors became perceived as immoral places that led young girls astray, enticing them down a path that inexorably led to ill repute and prostitution. This connection between ice-cream parlors and wickedness was so explicit by the late nineteenth century that some areas banned the sale of ice-cream sodas on Sundays.[17] What the temperance people sensed was that the soda shops provided a publicly sanctioned space for overt indulgence between men and women.

The tensions between indulgence and decorum were also evident in the way candy was marketed at around the same time. From the 1890s, ads depicted women in bare-shoulder blouses smiling provocatively over their shoulders and touching a small piece of candy to their seductively parted lips. However, the ads combined these lusty pictorial images with slogans that stressed the innocence of the indulgence. Various candy companies made "Purity" their motto. Whitman's Candies ads touted heavenly images of angels seated in a box of chocolates that appeared suspended in midair. The message was clear: in eating candy, the modern woman might indulge in sensuous pleasures but could also be pure at the very same time.[18]

Food and Guilt

Perhaps part of the appeal of coffee cafés is that, like the messages conveyed by the early candy ads, they promote a feeling of innocent indulgence. The fat being consumed is, after all "only a drink." And, like the ice-cream parlors of a hundred years ago, coffee cafés provide a space where this kind of pure indulgence can occur in a relaxed, clean-cut, mixed-sex environment.

Both the men and the women I was seeing in Seattle coffee cafés nearly all indulged in cream. One barista told me that customers regularly ordered a low-fat or skimmed milk drink and then added cream later from the cream thermos that most coffee cafés keep for customers' use next to the sugar and napkins. He said that customers often hid their cups behind the condiment table as they poured away. I didn't believe him, so he made me sit nearby until, about a quarter of an hour later, a plump man in shorts came and did just that. The barista laughed and thumbed his nose at me.

Customers who spoke with me were quite aware of why they came to the coffee café, and they were explicit about their desire to indulge. In fact, that was the exact word many of them used. "Coffee cafés are about indulging yourself," customers told me as they picked up the cream thermos. Jenny, a barista in an area of Seattle known as the University District, told me that student customers often spoke of their visits to the coffee café as being a "daily indulgence" that they carefully regulated. It appeared that they thought of "indulgence" as something "bad" that could be permitted in small doses, thereby limiting its effects and simultaneously allowing them to think of other spaces and other activities as "'good," through which they could recover so they could be "bad" again.

In another coffee café, I saw the barista, Kelly, serve five people in a row, who ordered skimmed milk drinks and then asked for whipped cream. I asked Kelly about this and she offered her theory, based on two years experience at the coffee bar: "They get uncomfortable. They wanted something rich, but they hold back in the drink. Then they're not satisfied with the drink, so they have to put the fat on top to richen it up, wanting and not wanting it. They're embarrassed."

Kelly's colleague Mike agreed with her. "We sell two percent the most, and a lot of nonfat," he told me. "But then people add fat. I think it's psychological. We are rewarded for eating healthy, but coffee isn't really healthy anything, so this is sort of middle-of-the-road. In coffee they can indulge, they can commit a little sin, do a little naughty thing, a bit of a taboo thing."

I was getting a bit perplexed with all this contradiction, so I began asking customers directly if they felt guilty when they drank cream. With only a few exceptions, almost everyone initially responded, often with some defiance, that no, they did not. Then, almost immediately, these same people would justify their lack of guilt or reverse their first statement.

"No, I don't feel guilt," a man in running clothes said. Then he paused. "If I weren't as active as I am, I guess I'd feel more. And I don't come in here so much, and I don't drink cream at home. I only allow myself to do this sometimes."

Another man, heavyset, in his forties, and wearing a suit, gave another perspective. "No," he said when I asked him if he felt guilty ordering his low-fat caramel mocha. "Smoking, yes. Fat is much less evil. We are designed to have fat. It's a marketing thing convincing us not to want fat, to fit into clothes that are too small for you."

I asked the same question to a woman in a fake fur jacket sitting in the chair beside me, waiting for her drink. "No, definitely not." Then when her frothy drink arrived, she turned to me again. "Well, sometimes," she added. "I think about my weight more than my husband. I guess I associate *eating* cream with weight gain." She then left in a hurry.

The finely tuned guilt, repression, and desire that emerged when I talked to customers seemed to contribute to the conflicted statements I encountered in these Seattle coffee cafés.

Forty of the fifty customers I directly observed took some sort of cream with their beverages. Five of the other ten drank what they all described to me as "creamy soy milk." The numbers were consistent for men and women, crossing all age groups. The numbers of men and women who used cream and whipped cream were about equal. Baristas told me that, if anything, men appeared more embarrassed in the eating of cream than were the women.

"I used to think there was a difference between what men and women drank," one barista told me. But, he said, these earlier observations were influenced by the fact that a few years earlier many more male than female customers had frequented the café. That had changed and now the numbers seemed to him to be about equal. And, he said, "I think men are just as self-conscious about eating cream and fat—maybe more."

Most customers, both men and women, were very clear that they did not permit the indulgence of the coffee café in other spaces of their lives, and certainly not at home. Being in the coffee café gave them a public space where indulgence was sanctioned and where they could escape from the control they tried to maintain in the rest of their lives. One seventeen-year-old woman said, "This is my real indulgence for the day. If not cream, then whipped cream. This is the only place I can drink real cream—just pour it on. For me, morning food is sweet and about fat. In the coffee shop I use butter for breakfast and eat pastries." Another man said that at home he eats only olive oil "and fats like that." At the coffee café, however, he always had cream. A man sitting nearby told me, "I look at the back of packages and if it has too much fat, I don't buy it. But here, I go on binges. Because I deserve it."

Deserve it? I asked myself. Why? Clearly, it seemed, because he needed a reward for his self-denial. And if no one else was going to reward him, then he would do it himself.

So, after all this, is the question of why we pour our conflicting attitudes of indulgence and restraint into the same cup of coffee answered? As I ponder the question now, sitting as I am at my favorite coffee café, all I can do is smile. I broke my ankle recently, so I hobbled here rather than coming my usual way, which is flushed from a brisk bike ride.

"Scone?" My barista friend Eric asked me when I had reached the counter.

"No, no," I replied, slightly scandalized. "I can't have a scone when I'm not getting exercise from riding my bike. No. No more scones until the ankle's healed."

Eric handed me my coffee and passed me the 2-percent from farther down the counter. I looked at him. He looked at me. A pause. Then I hobbled to the end of the counter and poured myself some half-and-half.

Chaos

Mark Graham

On a low table next to his bedroom window, Matthew has a framed close-up photograph of himself and a sheep he met in a field. (He has had to put up with a lot of teasing about his relationship to his woolly companion.) The photograph was taken on a sunny autumn day on a farm in England. Matthew's face is round, almost babyish, with ruddy cheeks, and he has thick strawberry-blond hair and a lush blond mustache. The picture is only ten years old, but the Matthew of today is almost unrecognizable from the Matthew in the photograph. When I first saw it,

I wasn't even sure it was him. It took an effort of imagination on my part to rebuild the Matthew I knew into the younger and much "fatter" Matthew in the picture. Today his moustache is gone and he has shaved his head, since his hair is thinning. But these are not the most obvious changes. His nose is now much thinner and sharper than in the photograph, where it appears quite round and snub. His cheeks are now sunken, and his eyes seem lost in their wide sockets. Matthew's skin is stretched taut over his face. This accentuates his now very visible bone structure. Matthew's appearance is caused by a condition called lipodystrophy.

The term *lipodystrophy* is a general medical term that refers to abnormal changes in fat metabolism and distribution. It is derived from the Greek for fat (*lipos*), bad (*dus-*), and nourishment (*trophia*), to give us *lipo-dys-trophy*. In Matthew's case the condition is caused by the treatment used to fight HIV. This treatment, called Highly Active Antiretroviral Therapy (HAART), or "Combination Therapy," began to be used in 1996, after the results of trials showed that certain combinations of anti-HIV drugs were effective in holding the virus in check.

Only a year after this new form of therapy had begun to be used, it became clear that something was wrong. Some people on HAART began to develop visible changes in their body fat, including the gaining of what doctors call "central" or visceral fat behind the abdominal muscles and around vital organs. The fat that gets deposited here is hard, unlike the soft subcutaneous fat found just under the skin. A layer of fat can also develop between the shoulder blades and across the back of the neck. This is unsightly and can make lying down uncomfortable as well as cause headaches. People sometimes call this layer of fat the "buffalo hump." In women, this fat can deposit in the breasts and cause them to enlarge and harden.

In addition to causing weight gain, HAART can also cause fat loss. This is another form of lipodystrophy known as lipo*atrophy*. Sufferers of lipoatrophy experience a loss of subcutaneous fat from the face, especially the temporal area and cheeks. This loss of fat results in a gaunt, emaciated appearance like Matthew's. The "owl look" is how one person described lipoatrophy when he, like many others, remarked on the irony in the use of treatments that keep people alive—who, in many cases, lead relatively normal lives—but leave some looking as though they were in the advanced stages of AIDS, even though they've never developed it. Fat is also lost from the limbs, making the arms and legs look thin and lined with prominent veins. Sometimes fat gain and fat loss occur in the same person.

The exact causes of lipodystrophy are still not known. Some researchers point to a class of drugs called protease inhibitors (PIs) as the culprit. Basically, PIs make it difficult for the body to mop up excess fat. The bloated stomach caused by visceral fat has been dubbed the "protease paunch" or "Crix belly" because it was first noted in people on Crixivan, one of the first and most widely used PIs. Another class of drugs called nucleoside reverse transcriptase inhibitors (NRTIs) may also be to blame because they interfere with the way cells produce energy. It may be that long-term HIV infection is also a factor.

While scientists try to figure all this out, one thing is very clear: fat is complicated. It isn't merely the domain of dieters and aesthetes. I discovered this while researching gays and consumption in Sydney. Although I knew what lipodystrophy was before embarking on the study, it was talking to Matthew about its consequences for his food consumption that led me to "fat." I soon became fascinated—and horrified—by the dizzying complexity of fat, and the ironic and sometimes cruel part it plays in the lives of people with HIV/AIDS.

Fat Trouble

Fat has always played a prominent role in the AIDS pandemic. One of the first names for the syndrome in African countries was "Slim," a reference to the wasting effects of myriad infections. When the acronym AIDS first appeared in the early 1980s, there was a dieting product of the same name on sale in the U.K. The diet drug Aids soon disappeared from supermarket shelves once tasteless jokes about its exaggerated effectiveness became common. AIDS often results in difficulties in eating, because it brings with it a host of oral, stomach, and intestinal infections that affect appetite, ingestion, digestion, absorption, and excretion.[1] The body, which already needs extra energy to fight HIV itself and other infections, rapidly becomes undernourished, and this leads to the wasting that became one of the most recognizable signatures of AIDS.

Since the 1980s, community self-help publications in many countries have devoted considerable attention to HIV/AIDS and nutrition. One deliberately outrageous but also serious gay magazine called the *Diseased Pariah News* contained a regular column entitled "GET FAT, don't die!" During the 1990s the "GET FAT, don't die!" column published recipes that flaunted dietary constraints on fat and gleefully advised its readers to eat, eat, and eat even more in order to put on weight. "Mmm-mmm! Feel those arteries harden! Serve with whipped cream," one of the columns advised its readers. Another column, in 1993, told readers that "the serum cholesterol of HIVers tends to be significantly lower than our seronegative comrades, so there is little worry about arteriosclerosis twenty years down the road."[2] Only four years later, however, warnings about alarmingly high cholesterol levels caused by HAART had already begun to appear.

HAART is usually begun when a person's CD4 cell levels drop to a point where the immune system may be compromised. (CD4 cells are the conductors of the immune system and the cells HIV infects and kills.) When enough of these cells are destroyed, the immune system stops responding to infections, leaving the person at risk of developing AIDS. Once the therapy begins, there is no turning back. The treatment schedules are very strict and must be adhered to without fail. If treatment does stop, there is a risk of developing viruses that are resistant to the drugs, and, hence, the risk of AIDS increases. Sticking to the treatment is often not easy, as HAART is a punishing chemical assault on HIV, and shrapnel from this assault affects the entire body. The drugs used can cause problems of their own, including anemia, mouth ulcers, dizziness, muscle soreness, changes in taste perception, diarrhea, intestinal problems including nausea and bloatedness, skin conditions, painful neurological complications, and liver and kidney problems.

On top of all these problems, there is also the need for people with HIV to think in terms of fat. For some people fat becomes important as soon as they start taking the drugs. Some of the drugs that are taken as part of HAART must be taken either in the absence of, or together with, fat. The reason for this is that fat helps the body absorb the medications. This could mean eating scrambled eggs, a baked potato with cheese, a hamburger with fries, a bacon sandwich smothered in mayonnaise, chocolate, or full-fat yogurt together with the drugs. A problem is that eating fatty food so that you can take your medicine pumps cholesterol into your body when the levels may already be sky-high. Matthew went through a period when he ate a fried egg every morning to help his medication. Most mornings he felt nauseous and had to force down the egg, even though it made him want to vomit.

Matthew received advice from a dietician about the kinds of food he should eat and the kinds he should avoid. Matthew is an accountant by profession, but nowadays he is also a lipoaccountant who counts and calculates fat intake as a matter of course. After several years, the restrictions on his diet have passed from being a complex puzzle to being an annoyance he has learned to live with. He has been passionate about food for as long as he can recall. He used to spend hours in the kitchen preparing lavish dishes rich in butter and cream, and he ate just about anything that had once had a pulse. All that has changed. Matthew has to contend with both severe lipoatrophy *and* very high cholesterol levels. To combat his lipoatrophy he has tried several herbal remedies but had to stop because of the risk that they would interfere with his medication. Instead of dubious remedies, he now eats food high in calories and low in animal fats, including lots of pasta. He has started to cook dishes that contain lots of vegetables, fruit, and fish. He no longer eats red meat and he avoids high-fat cheeses. The meat has not been a huge sacrifice, but for a cheese freak like Matthew, having to abstain from a runny wedge of ripe Brie with a glass (or, alas, a bottle) of red wine has been a real effort. Alcohol contributes to high triglyceride levels and should be drunk in moderation. Matthew regards this advice as horrific—unspeakable, really—but unfortunately sound.

Having to say no to fat has stolen some of his enjoyment of food. But it isn't only the pleasures of eating that fat chaos steals.

The photograph with the sheep is the only one Matthew has on display in his apartment. He has removed all the others, because they are too painful to him. Like most other people, though, he does have another photograph of himself that he has to show from time to time: namely, his passport picture. Matthew does not need to renew his current passport for several years. But when I first met him, he was toying with the idea of getting a new one with an up-to-date photograph in it. Matthew is an Australian citizen, so entry back into the country after a trip abroad ought not to have been a problem. During a trip to Europe he hadn't experienced any difficulties with immigration, but the passport controller at Sydney airport was leery. She kept staring at the picture, then at Matthew, then back at the picture. Finally she asked him when the photograph had been taken. Matthew told her that it was three years old. Still looking unsure, she had handed him back his passport and reluctantly let him through.

Matthew wasn't sure why the incident had upset him, but it had. Maybe it was because a passport is supposed to prove identity, not call it into question. Or maybe it was because the doubt on the face of the immigration official was a confirmation that he was no longer the person he had once been.

When Matthew started to develop lipodystrophy, he was the only person he knew who had the condition. At the time few people actually realized what lipodystrophy was. Matthew first noticed the loss of fat in his face. As his cheeks started to sink, he spent more and more time in front of the mirror, anxiously poring over his face. The first thing he did in the morning was stare into the mirror even before the sleep was out of his eyes. He suspected that the medication might be the culprit but tried to convince himself that it was just stress or tiredness, or maybe weight loss from all the vomiting and diarrhea. The problem was that he also started to develop a protease paunch and was faced with the problem of explaining how he could be gaining weight around his middle while losing it in his face. Now, of course, he knows the answer, but back in 1997 there was plenty of time for his imagination to run riot.

This is still true today for anyone who starts HAART. Are those simply love handles developing? Are they soft and doughy like real love handles or are they hard and taut? Might it be because of too much food over Christmas or too little time at the gym? Or is it the start of a protease paunch? Is that new wrinkle next to the eye just a sign of aging or is it lipoatrophy?

Matthew's lipodystrophy progressed quite rapidly, and for some time he was, he says, the only person on Oxford Street, the hub of Sydney's gay district, who looked as though he had lipodystrophy. Now there are more people, mostly men, who show signs of the condition. Seeing other similarly afflicted people was almost a relief for Matthew. But even today he admits that he is still slightly embarrassed when he meets anyone with severe lipodystrophy. He feels as though he should acknowledge them in some way: "give a sign of recognition" and "show that we have this in common, even if we probably don't have anything else in common." But meeting or even sometimes just seeing another person with lipodystrophy can be an unwelcome reminder. "You can be sitting there at a café on Oxford Street, not thinking of anything special or chatting with a friend, and then you're reminded of how you look," he told me.

Another friend of mine, Steve, is in his early thirties and

works in a marketing company. He is a fitness addict and has trained regularly at the gym for many years. He is tall and has the build of a world-class athlete. His dark good looks are inherited from his Greek father. Before lipoatrophy Steve looked a bit like a young Tony Curtis, only even more handsome. He likes to run, and at least two or three mornings a week he gets up extra early to go out jogging before work. Steve has severe facial lipoatrophy, but he has managed to maintain most of his body mass. He attributes this to all the gym work he did before and since he began treatment. His legs are still powerful but thin because they lack subcutaneous fat. The lack of subcutaneous fat on his arms gives him very high muscle definition and prominent veins—a kind of wiry Iggy Pop look. Bodybuilders aspire to the kind of muscle definition Steve has, but now he sees it as a curse. His big muscles compensate to some extent for his lack of fat, but the hard training that built them burns up the fat in his face and makes it look even thinner. Steve can't build up face muscles to conceal his facial lipoatrophy. Nor has he managed to maintain his muscular "bubble butt." He laments, "My butt used to be one of my best features, but not anymore!" No amount of gym works seems able to bring it back into shape. "I never thought I would want a fat arse!" he admits, but it is fat he needs to make it rounder, and it is fat that Steve lacks.

Lipoatrophy hasn't only stolen Steve's cute butt; it has also taken away much of his sex appeal. Since developing lipodystrophy, Steve spends less time in the bars in Sydney and more time sitting in cafés drinking caffe lattes made with soy milk, to keep down his cholesterol. He doesn't hide the fact that he is slightly bitter over the way other gay men now look at him. Gone are the days when he could pick up virtually any guy he wanted. His lipoatrophy has led to a painful reevaluation of his life as a sexually active gay man. But it is not only his appearance as such that has reduced his sex appeal. Although Steve's face is gaunt, he is certainly not ugly, and it is still obvious that he was once extremely handsome. His own explanation for the sharp decline in his sex life is that lipoatrophy makes his HIV status *too* obvious. It is not so much a question of him being HIV positive: he has had sex on many occasions with men who knew about his HIV status and who simply took the usual safe-sex precautions. Rather, there is something about what he calls his increasingly "skull-like" appearance that puts people off and makes them think twice about having sex with him.

Matthew tells a different story. "I've never been that good-looking," he told me. "Not the kind that turns head or everybody wants. I can't compete with the muscle queens at Mardi Gras. Not that I cared. So I've never gone out certain that I'd get somebody. I mean, I hoped I would, but I never took it for granted. I can honestly say that I get as much sex now as before." Lipodystrophy has proved to be a great leveler for Matthew. Many men who were out of his league in the looks department are now available, even if they are not as good-looking as they used to be. He has met other gay men with lipodystrophy at HIV-positive evenings at Sydney bars and through his voluntary work. And he is quick to point out that not all HIV-negative men discriminate against HIV-positive men, even if they have lipodystrophy.

Lipoliteracy

In fat-obsessed cultures we are all "lipoliterates" who "read" fat for what we believe it tells us about a person. This includes not only their moral character but also their health. People with lipodystrophy do not escape these readings. On the contrary, they live in constant anxiety about them.

Matthew experienced such readings at his job. Coworkers knew that he had been ill and why, but clients had started to stare at him. He felt uncomfortable, and it was obvious that they did too. Eventually, Matthew left his job and received an early sick-leave pension. It was a relief to escape the stares. Now he is less concerned by people looking at him, but at the time his self-confidence disappeared as quickly as his fat.

Steve often wonders how people read his appearance when he is out jogging. It has occurred to him that they might suspect that he is suffering from an eating disorder. He finds the idea of being confused with someone who is anorexic grimly amusing, given the huge amount of calories he consumes in order to be able to manage his jogging and his training regime at the gym. Because he has the owl look, they might suspect AIDS. But people with AIDS don't normally jog effortlessly around Sydney Harbor at seven thirty in the morning. Steve's emaciated face but muscular body send out different signals that are hard for those who see them to interpret.

After ten years of being HIV-positive, Greg, who is in his late twenties and works with computers, has only just had to start combination therapy as his CD4 cells began to reach critically low levels. He is worried that he will develop signs of lipodystrophy in the near future. But it's not just losing his looks that concerns him. Over a decade ago he spent time as an exchange student in New York and has friends there he hasn't seen for years, although he has regular e-mail contact with them. He can't really afford to visit them now, but if he puts off visiting for another year, which is his plan, he worries that signs of lipoatrophy may appear. This could make him an easy target for immigration officials who are lipoliterate and can recognize the telltale signs of lipoatrophy. A quick search of luggage will turn up anti-HIV drugs. (They have to be taken every day: you can't leave them at home without running risks of developing resistance.) U.S. immigration law does not allow HIV-positive foreigners to enter the country, even as tourists. What this means is that "fat" has placed Greg in a situation where he sees himself in a race against time.

Men like Steve and Greg think a great deal about how they are or will be read by others who recognize the signs of lipodystrophy or know nothing about the condition. Other gay men in and around Oxford Street are sufficiently well informed to recognize it and distinguish it from AIDS. However, gay men can make their own errors of lipoliteracy. A naturally gaunt face can be mistaken for lipoatrophy. This situation is reminiscent of the 1980s during the early years of the AIDS pandemic, when a loss of weight had to be avoided at all costs because people suspected it was a sign of AIDS.

Both Steve and Greg are openly gay at work, and their workmates know about their HIV. Others have never told friends and kin that they are HIV-positive. In some cases they haven't even revealed that they are gay. They may have lived for years dreading the day when illness would force them to tell others about their sexuality and their HIV/AIDS. At first, the new treatments seemed to hold out the promise that they would never need to do this. But what happens when lipodystrophy starts to become obvious and people start to ask questions? It may not be AIDS that "outs" them; HAART does that, and its instrument is fat.

As the number of people with signs of lipodystrophy grows, new kinds of speculation and even discrimination based on a lack of fat, not the presence of too much fat, could appear. None other than Michael Jackson found himself on the receiving end of a reading in the fall of 2003. An article in the weekly scandal sheet *The Globe* speculated that Jackson's gaunt appearance at the Radio Music Awards on October 27, where he received the Humanitarian Award, might be the result of treatments for HIV.

Fighting Fat

So what are the options for people in the same situation as Matthew, Steve, and perhaps someday Greg? This is where things get even more complicated and frustrating. As Steve has discovered, you can train hard to build muscle to compensate for lost fat, but you risk getting an even thinner face. Human growth hormone is another option for building muscles, but it, too, causes fat loss in the face. Because he is familiar with gym culture, Steve knows all about the drug but also about the possible side effects, and has decided not to try it. As Matthew can tell you, eating more fats and calories to replace fat you've lost worsens high blood-sugar and cholesterol levels.

Another option is to redistribute fat. But in the case of Steven and Matthew, redistributing subcutaneous fat isn't much of an option as they have so little fat to harvest. A buffalo hump isn't a problem for Steve or Matthew, but some people who have developed one try liposuction. Unfortunately, the humps have a tendency to grow back.

If real fat is in short supply and what you do have will not do what you want it to, then what about fake fat? This is becoming a common strategy for people with facial lipoatrophy. There are several fat substitutes on the market with names like New-Fill, Fascian, and AlloDerm. They don't always work well, but so far they seem the best option for many people. However, they can be expensive. Matthew dislikes the idea of being injected, so a fat substitute is not for him. Steve has considered plastic surgery but hasn't done anything about it yet. Greg, however, says that he will beat a path to the door of the nearest clinic, should the day ever come when he develops lipoatrophy.

The most drastic option for someone with lipodystrophy is to stop HAART altogether or to refuse to begin the treatment. I know one man in his mid-thirties in Sydney who really needs to start combination therapy now. His dread of developing lipodystrophy is so strong that he has ignored his doctors, who are imploring him to begin treatment, and he is prepared to risk coming down with a serious infection, or death.

Just how dependent we are on fat for our individual appearance was brought home to me by Gareth and David. Gareth and David have been a couple for years. They were both diagnosed HIV-positive and started HAART together. There is something very touching about seeing them together. Pre-lipodystrophy, they looked rather unlike each other. In addition to being ten years younger, Gareth was also much stockier than David. Now that lipoatrophy has carved away their fat, they look more and more like brothers. They have always dressed similarly, even though they couldn't share each other's clothes because of the weight difference. Now they can because they have almost the same build: each has a protease paunch and a bit of a hump. But even their faces have grown, or rather shrunk, alike. Looking at Gareth and David, you realize just how much one's individual appearance relies on fat. Take it away and we really do start to lose some of our individuality. It's under our fat, not only under our skin, that we are all the same.

Chaos

Like most people, I once thought of "fat" as a fairly simple substance, a straightforward concept. Admittedly, I could make a distinction between saturated and polyunsaturated fats, and I knew a little about cholesterol, but that was all. Coming to know people with lipodystrophy has changed this. What becomes very clear as soon as you begin thinking about lipodystrophy is that fat is a very complicated phenomenon. For men like Matthew, Steve, and Greg, fat becomes a cruel, malicious joker that betrays them, refuses to do what they want it to do, and has a mind of its own. For these men, fat has fragmented into a menacing myriad of different substances with different characteristics and consequences for their bodies and health.

Our ways of describing fat and the use of fatty metaphors, at least in English, reveal an ambiguity that is almost invisible in our lipophobic times, when we focus almost exclusively on the downside of fat. Yes, fat can be a sign of excess and inertia, but it can also indicate growth (as in to "fatten up" after illness) and denote prosperity—at least a few centuries ago. "The fat of the land" describes the good things in life as opposed to the "lean times," when they are in short supply. Even the medical leaflets on lipodystrophy talk of "good" and "bad" cholesterol. Yet, both types are essential for health. The cultural messages that bombard us daily are equally contradictory. Turn on the television and you are told to indulge yourself with fatty foods one minute and to diet and stay slim the next.

People with lipodystrophy aren't just faced with these contradictory consumer messages; they embody them. Their bodies are battlegrounds. As they lose and gain fat in unwelcome and uncontrollable ways, people with lipodystrophy are living a nightmare all of us in the fat-obsessed West to some extent dread: fat turned into chaos.

Spam

Julia Harrison

Spam, Spam, Spam, Spam, Spam, Spam, Spam, Spam, lovely Spam! Wonderful Spam!

Vikings in a rousing chorus, *Monty Python's Flying Circus*

Palm trees swaying in a humid breeze. Pineapples. Sugarcane. Hula girls and leis. Handsome young men with surfboards. Gorgeous beaches and breathtaking mountains. Bubbling volcanoes. Ukuleles. Don Ho, floral patterned shirts, "Tiny Bubbles." Aloha!

Muumuus. Mai tais. Spam.

Yes, Spam.

It may seem startling, and it certainly clashes with the other stereotypical images of Hawai'i that are so dear to many non-Hawaiians. But Spam is as Hawaiian as . . . well, as apple pie is to mainland Americans.

According to the makers of Spam, "Hawai'i is the nation's biggest per capita Spam consumer, with an annual consumption rate of more than four cans per Hawaiian."[1] Spam, that humble, inexpensive canned meat, made largely from chopped pork with a bit of ham and "secret spices" (which we know from other, un-official, Spam Web sites are salt, sugar, and sodium nitrate) is not what most people think of when they conjure up images of Hawai'i. Instead, the islands are more likely to be associated with sensual pleasures and hedonistic indulgences—things a bit diffi-cult to reconcile with a can of Spam.

The short answer to why Hawaiians eat so much Spam is be-cause Spam is portable, cheap, has a long shelf life, and is a great emergency food when a hurricane strikes. It can also be adapted to a dazzling range of cultural and ethnic tastes, and Hawaiians have made the most of this. Go to Hawai'i and you can enjoy Spam wontons, Spam and poi, Spam sushi, and Spam *musubi*, which is Japanese rice in a rectangular block with a slice of Spam on top, wrapped in a strip of seaweed. Delicacies like these, rich in fat—or, as locals would say, with grease—makes them truly *ono* (delicious) to island tastes.

But the long answer to Spam's popularity in Hawai'i is much more complicated.

Spam in History

Spam is an industrial food. It is mass-produced and considered by many to be offensive to refined sensibilities. Full of preservatives, it is always guaranteed to slither from its tin, thanks to the yellowish-white fat that coats its pink rectangular shape. Originally called Spiced Ham, Spam was first produced in 1937 by the George Hormel meat-processing company based in Austin, Minnesota. The company, which had been in business since the 1890s, held a competition in that year to come up with a name for their new product, a name that would be as "creative as the taste" of the canned meat. The winning entry combined the *sp* from *spiced* with the *am* from *ham*, leading to the memorable *Spam*.[2] Spam became Hormel's most successful product, an accomplishment fueled by its adoption as a staple in the Allied Forces' rations in World War II. The American military buildup in and around Hawai'i after the attack on Pearl Harbor not only brought tens of thousands of soldiers, but it also flooded the islands with Spam.

But Hawai'i was not the only part of the United States where canned meat made an appearance. Canned meats had become a regular part of the diet of many ordinary mainland North Americans by the end of the nineteenth century. These meats provided readily available sources of protein in areas that lacked refrigeration and regular access to fresh foods.[3] In second half of the twentieth century, however, foods like Spam began to lose their appeal on the mainland. The electricity grid spread across the continent, thereby providing most of the population with access to refrigeration. Increasing urbanization brought large-scale grocery stores, which in turn offered consumers a wider array of foods. Processed foods began to evoke the prosaic rather than the sophisticated. The flusher wallets of the burgeoning middle classes in the post–World War II era allowed them to opt for fresh foods—even if "fresh" often meant "freshly frozen." Cheaper canned staples such as Spam were left behind as the middle class pulled themselves up the social ladder. Eating Spam became symbolic of lower-class tastes.

This class-based taste shift accounts for what is now, in the twenty-first century, the very common usage of the term *Spam* to describe other products, and even concepts. For instance, the ubiquitous, unwelcome, often tawdry commercial messages that flood our e-mail accounts are called Spam, in honor of the Monty Python Spam skit in which patrons in a café can't escape Spam. (Every item on the menu contains Spam, including "lobster thermidor à crevette with a Mornay sauce served in a Provençale manner with shallots and aubergines garnished with truffle pâté, brandy, and with a fried egg on top and Spam.")[4] In general, Spam has come to denote anything that is mass-produced, trashy, and vulgar.

But not in all quarters. In Hawai'i, Spam has none of these connotations. Spam rapidly became central to the local diet during World War II, partly because of its ready availability and low cost but also because a local staple, fish, became scarce as a result of the American government's ban on offshore fishing following the bombing of Pearl Harbor. Spam became an unlikely "comfort" food, a staple with which people associated their successful struggle through hard times during the war. And over the years it just became part of the island tradition.[5]

Eating Grease

To the extent that non-Hawaiians think of Hawaiian food at all, they are likely to come up with fruits like pineapples or coconuts. Those who have actually visited Hawai'i may think of macadamia nuts. Beyond these particular foods, though, Hawai'i has never been noted for its cuisine. To the contrary.

Food historian Rachel Laudan begins her generally sensitive and thoroughly researched history-cum-recipe book on food in Hawai'i with a raised eyebrow: "Hawai'i's culinary heritage?" Until recently, Laudan writes, Hawaiian cuisine was represented outside Hawai'i as not much more than that "sweet and sour glop, pineapple in every dish, that Jim Dole and Trader Vic had persuaded the world was 'Hawaiian' or 'Polynesian' food."[6]

"Real"—or at least pre–colonial contact—island foods had included fish, shellfish, the root taro, sweet potato, breadfruit, sugarcane, seaweed, bananas, and yams, foods that are all too rare in the diets of many Hawaiians today. Rich, greasy pork was traditionally a food eaten only periodically, on ceremonial occasions. Today, though, it has become a staple, with consequences that are far from beneficial.[7] Ironically, the "sweet and sour glop, pineapple in every dish" was never actually part of the local diet. In fact, pineapple is not even indigenous to the islands; it was introduced in the early nineteenth century by the Spanish and developed as a commercial crop by mainland Americans. Tourists coming to the islands imagined that the exotic fruit must be an island staple. For this reason, after World War II it began to appear on the menus of the restaurants in tourist hotels.

Much of what I know about Hawai'i and Hawaiians comes from the time I spent working as an anthropologist at the Bishop

Museum in Honolulu. My colleagues patiently educated me about things Hawaiian during my stay there. For example, I was told that despite whatever else you may find curious or even annoying about your Chinese, Filipino, Japanese, or haole (the local word for a Caucasian mainlander) neighbor or in-law, acceptable island behavior did not include mocking what someone else ate—except in the most jovial way. I quickly learned that people often thought of themselves in terms of food. Some jokingly referred to local Hawaiians as "Heinz 57," as being as varied in ancestry and cultural traditions as the fifty-seven "varieties" of Heinz products made so famous as Heinz's advertising campaigns. In the nineteenth century, people from myriad cultural backgrounds were brought to Hawai'i to work as indentured laborers on the sugar and pineapple plantations. A close associate of mine at the museum schooled me in what she called the "salad bowl of Hawai'i" by telling me about her own ancestry, a combination of native Hawaiian, Portuguese, Filipino, Chinese, Japanese, haole, Korean, and even African American. She told me that people who were true islanders were a "little bit this, a little bit that . . . all mixed like a salad."

At work, we talked incessantly about food. Conversations around the lunch table, a place where some of my richest research was carried out, always seemed to be about food. We talked about what was *ono* (delicious) and what was not, what were island delicacies, what food should be served at the next museum function, and what island restaurants and eateries were worth a visit. Food was never far from our minds. Neither was it ever very far from our mouths. We always seemed to be eating.

My coworkers classified people into two types of eaters: those who eat "healthy" and those who eat "grease." As soon as people saw me nibbling away at my green salads during lunch, I was pegged as a healthy eater. It took me a while to understand that this designation was not particularly positive. It labeled me as someone who was definitely *not* from the islands.

Every day we would munch on doughnuts, leftover pizza, cake, potato chips, and other fatty snacks laid out in the department office. Around 11:45 a call would go up and down the hallway querying who wanted what for lunch. When we all reached some kind of agreement, one of us would go to collect a take-out order from a neighborhood eatery. Korean, Japanese, and Chinese fare were the most readily available choices. Sometimes a trip farther afield would be made for special treats, such as plate lunches from establishments such as Masu's Massive Plate Lunch, the most popular local eatery in Honolulu. I willingly began to join in these daily rituals. Fourteen months later I came home several pounds heavier. The extra weight was a testimony to the taste I had acquired for "grease."

For the locals I knew in Hawai'i, eating grease was about eating processed food, like Spam, foods that could then be "reprocessed" in order to adapt it to the varied culinary heritages of Hawai'i: fried, baked, steamed, marinated, wrapped in a wonton or barbecued. Grease did not include food in its "raw" state, such as Spam straight from the can. Instead, grease was food that was fully "cultured" by being transformed into some distinctive island fare. Many other foods categorized as grease were frequently just that: greasy. Portuguese doughnuts, Korean barbecue, Chinese chicken long rice, and *kalua* pork all have a very high fat content. In this way the local population almost claimed grease—claimed fat itself—as its own. The constant influx of tourists makes it difficult for islanders to feel that they are not mere "attractions" in their own homeland. They resist this designation in various ways. One place where I came to see this resistance was in their valorization of foods that no tourist would associate with Hawai'i. Grease is not what appeals to the nearly seven million tourists who come to the islands every year. For locals, consuming grease is never just mere sustenance; it is an act invested with a significant degree of culture and emotion.

Spam, here, is good grease. First of all, it is richly coated in fat. Keala Beamer, a local songwriter, poet, and collector of Spam haiku, offers this lovely ode:

> *Queasy, greasy SPAM*
> *Slithers without propulsion*
> *Across a white plate.*[8]

Openly enjoying Spam is an in-your-face response to tourists who see themselves as too sophisticated for Spam and who are baffled by its island popularity. Hawaiians find it amusing that Spam is considered tacky on the mainland. They know that mainlanders scoff at Spam, but they don't care: mainland disdain has not prevented Hawaiians from taking pride in finding Spam *ono*, tasty and delicious. Eating Spam conveys the message that locals, who are born in the islands and are connected emotionally and historically to them, are distinct from the powerful outside mainlanders and from the stereotypes that leave the impression that Hawaiian culture hardly extends beyond hula girls and Don Ho and his tiny bubbles.

Recently islanders have cranked up their enthusiastic championing of Spam by launching a three-day festival called SPAM JAM, which includes a contest to construct the "Great Wall of Spam" and to prepare the world's longest Spam *musubi*, which must measure 325 feet to establish a Guinness World Record. Staging these events in Waikiki, the infamous tourist mecca, is, as one newspaper reported, a way of exposing Hawai'i's culinary vice to the visiting public.[9]

During my first Halloween at the museum, a false-front "trick-or-treat street" had been set up in front of the main building for neighborhood children. All staff members were expected to dress up for the festivities. I wondered what dressing up for Halloween—yet another mainland American import to the islands—would mean in Hawai'i. In the end, the predictable witches, vampires, and ghosts appeared, but these were costumes donned largely by outsiders. Locals were much more imaginative, inventive, and original in their costumes. Knowing the local fascination with food, I guess I shouldn't have been surprised when Chicken Long Rice, *lau lau*, and Poi walked into the museum. Chicken Long Rice is a mixture of bean thread noodles and chicken; *lau lau* is a mixture of pork and salt fish steamed in taro leaves; poi is a paste made from taro root. All of these foods are local and all are *ono* to that palate. The costumes were simple yet readily recognizable. Strategic decorative elements included real taro leaves such as would wrap *lau lau,* and simulated pieces of onion, noodles, and chicken to denote Chicken Long Rice. Most strategically, however, the words FOR LOCALS ONLY were written in bold letters on the purple bag of poi.

Served the way they are preferred by a local palate—chicken with the skin on, pork wrapped so the fat cannot escape, and cool, tangy poi served with crisp fried Spam—these "costumed" foods brilliantly exemplify island grease. And it was fitting that it was the museum's staff, rather than its managers, who chose to dress up as local foods that exemplify or accompany island grease. These museum workers were not drawn from the elite ranks of island society. Museum staff were paid modest wages in a state with a very high cost of living. But even so, they were better off than those islanders who work in the tourist industry, which some claim has simply replaced the indentured servitude of the plantations. Foreign investors and the tourist industry determine much of what happens in the islands: where roads are built, what shoreline is saved, what reefs are protected, and how much water is available to local farmers. Locals today eat the foods that connect them to a history that is very different from that of those who come to search for an island paradise, or those who view it as a lucrative place for financial investment.

The Dark Side of Spam

In the early 1990s, I was startled to hear stories of families who lived in the campgrounds in the state parks because there was no other accommodation they could afford. Even these publicly owned spaces are few in number, since most of the good beach property is given over to luxury resorts and golf courses. The families who lived on the campgrounds worked at low-paying jobs, often in the tourist industry. The wages they earned did not allow them to buy a home or even pay the high rents in the islands. Every seven days—the length of time anyone is allowed to stay in one campsite in the state parks—these people packed up their tents and other belongings, moved outside the park gates for the night, and the next morning moved back for the next week. Spam enters the picture here because under these itinerant conditions, the food's long shelf life serves the same purpose as it did for those in earlier eras without electricity.

The fact that many Native Hawaiians—and here I am referring specifically to Hawai'i's aboriginal population—do not own land on the islands that were once theirs is one of the grim island realities of which most tourists remain blissfully ignorant. Many Native Hawaiians occupy the lowest rung of the socioeconomic ladder. How this troubling circumstance came into being is a complex story of deceit, bureaucratic bungling, and corporate greed on the part of the mainlanders and later of local politicians who came to control the islands. But it is also part of the story of how Spam became a staple in the diets of these people.

Spam and other examples of grease—even if they may taste good to locals, and even if they are important in symbolizing who is local and who is not—have a dark side, particularly for native Hawaiians. Many Native Hawaiians live well below the poverty line. They have the highest mortality rate on the islands. These health issues are often directly related to the fact that many Native Hawaiians are overweight, mirroring what many observers have noted for mainland Americans: the further down the socioeconomic scale you go, the more obese the population.[10] Inexpensive snack foods are also ready to eat, while fast-food chains provide the restaurant meals—high in fat—that poorer populations can afford. The troubling health consequences of incessant consumption of high-fat foods are now daily news in North America. Yet, Captain Cook, on his visits to Hawai'i in the late eighteenth century, specifically noted how healthy the Hawaiians looked. Even the big-bodied upper classes radiated health, Cook wrote. The large size of chiefly and noble bodies reflected the prosperity of their subjects. They signified that these people were able to feed their masters well from the foods they harvested from the land and the water. Eighteenth-century Hawaiians ate a very different—and far healthier—diet than the one that is consumed today.

This story has changed, however. The contemporary diet of

Spam and other beloved island grease has turned the generous Hawaiian body into one that is unhealthy. Native Hawaiian sovereignty activist Mililani Trask has suggested that unless dramatic changes are made in the life circumstances of her people, specifically in their diet, they will all die off in fifty to sixty years.[11] Native Hawaiians themselves are well aware of this prognosis. So why don't they simply change their diet? Why not give up the delights of foods such as Spam, especially if they're killing you?

The anthropologist Sidney Mintz, who studied the history of sugar, has argued that the development of the sweet tooth of the English working class in the eighteenth and nineteenth centuries emerged as a result of a conflation of cultural, economic, and political forces. A symbiosis of these forces produced the rotting teeth of English children for a very long time as well as the prosperity of many an English capitalist. They fueled an expanding empire, the exploitation of an available workforce, and the rapidly growing popularity for the sweetener among the English working class: sugar, along with tea, soon came to define the English character. Once a treat reserved for the rich, sugar sweetened the bitterness of both the workers' lives and their much-loved "cuppa tea." It also, incidentally—and lucratively, for their employers—prolonged the workers' energy and numbed their gnawing hunger pangs.[12]

Like sugar for the United Kingdom, Spam for the United States is one of those industrial foods that facilitated global expansion by providing a durable and portable food source for soldiers and laborers. For local Hawaiians, Spam also ironically became a symbol of resistance to those same powerful forces that came to dominate life in the islands. It arrived with mainland American colonists; it filled empty stomachs of island plantation laborers, just as sugar dulled the hunger pangs of the English factory worker. In addition, it was adaptable to myriad cuisines. A highly processed food when it was packed in the tin back in Austin, Minnesota, Spam slips out of the tin in Hawai'i as a raw ingredient to be shaped, or "cultured," to suit a wide variety of local tastes. Another reason for its popularity is that Spam became readily available at the same time that access to traditional food sources was progressively eliminated—when lands were taken over for plantations, tourist hotels, urban development, and other mainland projects in the islands.

To return to a diet more closely linked to that which native Hawaiians were eating when Cook arrived in Hawai'i will take an equally complex interweaving of culture, economics, and politics. Traditional foods need to become appreciated for being just as *ono* as Spam, and Native Hawaiians will also have to secure ready access to the lands and waters from which to harvest them. Reimagining traditional foods as *ono* is a fairly tall order because, as social historian Peter Stearns has observed, when people are denied many other satisfactions in their life, such as meaningful work or a place to permanently call home, they often turn to food as a source of satisfaction.[13]

If and when Native Hawaiians regain the title to their lands, no one imagines a return to a traditional lifestyle of centuries past. But activists and community workers are promoting the production and consumption of traditional foods as symbols of autonomy, sovereignty, and community pride. They hope that a reclaimed ownership to at least some of what once were were their native lands will result in regular consumption of more traditional, locally produced dietary staples.

The great French gastronome Jean Anthelme Brillat-Savarin

once famously remarked, "Tell me what you eat, and I will tell you what you are." People who identify as locals in Hawai'i live by Brillat-Savarin's dictum, setting themselves apart from mainlanders partly through their love of Spam and the desire for grease. But even as we champion events like SPAM JAM and applaud the consumption of Spam with attitude, one wonders if the consequences of a lifetime of eating grease will be the spoils of a sore winner.

Chasers

Matti Bunzl

Bustin' Apart at the Seams is a classic movie and a landmark in the history of American fat. Produced in 1992, it was the first commercial porn flick that featured chubby gay men having sex. The production value may have been "straight to video," with poor lighting and awkward camera movements. But that didn't matter to the many gay men who until then had only fantasized about such a visual spectacle. These were fantasies with a market potential, and Ritch Bergland, the producer of *Bustin' Apart at the Seams*, dutifully obliged these desires. Under the studio name

Maximum Density Productions, he proceeded to create a little industry of gay chubby porn, an industry that he also serviced with the magazine *Bulk Male*, a kind of *Playguy* for the chubby set.

One might think that a niche video like *Bustin' Apart at the Seams* would go unnoticed outside the world of gay fat porn aficionados. But not so. Over the years an entire group of scholars have found their way to Bergland's films and magazines. Writing from an emerging academic discipline known as Fat Studies, they have trained their collective eye on the subversive dimensions of what fans and analysts alike have come to call "chubby porn."

For these academics, chubby porn constitutes a political challenge to the fat phobia of contemporary culture. In an essay entitled "Life in the Fat Lane," for example, cultural critic Laura Kipnis highlights the American obsession with fat and the hysterical attempt to hide it from public view. She cites *Bustin' Apart at the Seams* and *Bulk Male* as potent forms of resistance in this context, defying as they do the assignment of fat sexuality to "visual leper colonies."[1] "Fat porn's mission," she concludes, in language that is echoed by other scholars in Fat Studies, "is to bring fat out of the closet and deliver it up for public viewing."[2]

This interpretation of fat sexuality's defiant quality is powerful. It captures the genuine disruption that a copy of *Bulk Male* constitutes when it is placed alongside the trim, muscled gladiatorlike hunks that appear on the covers of all the other magazines that you can find on the porn rack of your local gay bookstore. It also accounts for the feeling of empowerment that is generated during what are called "Convergences," organized meetings of chubby gay men and those who like them. There is a social movement catering to this group: Girth & Mirth. Girth & Mirth goes back to mid-1970s San Francisco, home of the first club by that name. From there, the concept spread to other

American cities and then to Europe. Staged across North America and Europe since the 1980s, these meetings bring together hundreds of sexy chubbies whose public appearance flouts the common stereotype that fat people are supposed to be lonely and isolated. Today, Convergences are held annually on both sides of the Atlantic. Hosting duties shift from one Girth & Mirth club to another and, hence, from city to city.

Girth & Mirth, Convergences, and the pornographic depiction of chubby sex surely are subversive challenges to a society that hates and fears fat. But at the same time, we perhaps ought to be wary of a certain romantic view of chubby porn as part and parcel of a kind of fat emancipation. Let's face it: cultural artifacts like *Bustin' Apart at the Seams* and *Bulk Male* are not produced by political activists like those who work with the National Association to Advance Fat Acceptance (NAAFA). They are produced by commercial entrepreneurs. Chubby porn is part of an economy of sex that exists to the extent that it succeeds in catering to the desire to consume—that is, to buy—more chubby porn.

Now, to say this is not to say that pornography is bad and nothing more than an egregious symptom of capitalist exploitation. Not at all. Instead, the point is to encourage us to look a bit more seriously at the libidinal logic of chubby porn: at how chubby porn is structured, and at what messages it conveys. *Bustin' Apart at the Seams* may well undermine and challenge our fat-phobic culture as *form*, since it represents bodies and desires that are normally kept hidden from view. But if we only consider form, we would miss the film's actual *content*. And if we look closely at that—at how chubby porn is staged and portrayed— then what we see is a far more complex and less obviously "progressive" design.

That design caters to the desires of the "chaser." *Chaser* is a term for a gay man who is sexually attracted to fat men. As such, chasers are the counterparts to chubbies. The chubbies are not their equals, however. On the contrary, the chubby/chaser relationship is a complicated one, fraught with divergent desires and marked by inequality. Ultimately, these differences make *Bustin' Apart at the Seams* less about the emancipation of fat than the satisfaction of a particular erotic preference.

What does this mean? Let's start at the beginning. In its basic structure, *Bustin' Apart at the Seams* closely adheres to the conventional format of commercial gay pornography. For one, the flick is not exactly encumbered by narrative and plot. Instead, it features seven men who, in the inimitable language of gay porn, do "what cums naturally." This happens in four separate scenes, the first three of which showcase couples who run through the usual repertoire of sex acts, and the last depicting a somewhat tepid orgy involving all seven performers. The setting for the wordless action is a gymnasium; the music playing in the background is strictly canned.

Pretty standard gay porn, in other words. But the twist, of course, is in the size of the men. Well, not all of them, actually. *Bustin' Apart at the Seams* does feature a number of performers whose body shape could have landed them in any mainstream studio production. But they are paired with a few big boys who, before the film's 1992 release, were not found anywhere in gay pornography. Those men range in size from the upper-200- to the mid-300-pound range.

The highlight and centerpiece of *Bustin' Apart at the Seams* comes quite early, in the second scene of the film. While the first sequence presents a bland whirlpool encounter between a chub and chaser, it is the second scene that truly delivers. Simply put, that segment is a chaser's wet dream. Literally.

Reproduced with permission of Richard Bergland and Maximum Density Productions

The action features two massive men, Ben Rice and Harald Wilke, going at it. Bearded, round, and at about 300 pounds each, they are what chasers like to call "proportionate," an adjective that denotes exactly the right kind of curvature: a body of heft that is also contoured, a softness without uncontrollable sprawl. With one of them tall and hairy (Ben) and the other one short and smooth (Harald), and featuring a long beard (Harald) versus a short beard (Ben), they also bring a nice variety to the film.

Within the world of Girth & Mirth, there are numerous terms that convey finer distinctions of body type. An important distinction is the difference between chubs and superchubs, one that is hard to describe in absolute terms. In practice, a majority of chasers are primarily attracted to "proportionate" men, or chubs whose physiques have dimensions from about five feet five inches/240 pounds to six feet three inches/350 pounds. Super-chubs are men with significantly greater weights, and there is a subset of chasers with a clear preference for them. A majority of chasers, however, would think of them as "fat." Ben and Harald are not fat. They are chubby—chubby pinups, at that.

The scene of Ben and Harald in *Bustin' Apart at the Seams* is the unquestionable highpoint of early gay chubby porn. Its crucial significance is that it features two large men. That Ben and Harald may also be chasers (which is a category of desire rather than physical stature) is less relevant here than the fact that the scene involves sex between two chubbies.

The reason this is so significant is because it reveals a simple truth about gay chubby porn: the object of the genre may be chubs, but its imagined viewer is a chaser. Chubbies who are not chasers themselves (that is, the vast majority) do not usually find scenes between men like Ben and Harald particularly appealing. To them, chubby porn only becomes sexually interesting if it features big men having sex with more conventionally handsome—and slim—chasers. In those cases, a chub might identify with the chubby in the video. But even that is quite rare in practice, because the overwhelming majority of chubs simply prefer "regular" gay porn.

Gay chubby porn, then, is not made for chubs. It is made for chasers—and by chasers. That it features chubby men, many of whom may genuinely enjoy the sex they have on camera, has little to do with chubby sexual emancipation. It has to do with their transformation into objects of desire.

To understand this more easily, think of the "lesbian" girl-on-girl scenes in straight pornography. The two women who have sex with each other in any of the ubiquitous "lesbian" scenes in straight porn may actually be enjoying their break from penile penetration. But the reason the scenes are there has nothing to do with their pleasure. What has to be satisfied is straight male logic—one that prizes the fantasy of a triangulated attraction between the objects of one's desire (triangulated in the sense that he desires them, and they desire one another, but they have sex with one another while they know he is watching because what they *really* desire is him).

So it is with gay chubby porn. Much like some female porn stars who appear with other women, men like Ben Rice and Harald Wilke may have a genuine attraction to other big men. But such personal desires are subordinate to gratifying the gaze of the chaser. It is his desire that gay chubby porn caters to, which is why sex between two slim men will never occur in a chubby porn flick. Sex between two slim men in a chubby porn flick would be as anathema as sex between two men would be in a straight porn flick.

"*Chaser* Is to *Chubby* as *Male* Is to *Female*"

All of this begins to reveal one of the most striking features not only of *Bustin' Apart at the Seams* but of the Girth & Mirth scene in general: its peculiar gendering. It may seem crude to suggest a formula like "*Chaser* is to *chubby* as *male* is to *female*," but it is a somewhat accurate assessment. Built into the chubby/chaser relationship are specific kinds of contrasts. For one, chubby and chaser are imagined, at least in their ideal-typical forms, as physical opposites—the former of "comfortable" size, the latter of notably smaller stature. Even more important, and suggested by their very name, chasers are seen as the active part of the pair, pursuing presumably passive chubbies in their quest for sexual fulfillment. There is a certain awareness of, and discomfort with, these connotations within the Girth & Mirth scene, and periodically, people in the scene express a desire for new terminology. In the late 1990s the terms *Big Man* (instead of *chub*) and *Admirer* (instead of *chaser*) were quite popular. These words were drawn from the language of heterosexual fat appreciation, in which there are categories like "Big Handsome Man" (BHM) as well as the "Fat Admirer (FA) of Big Beautiful Woman (BBW)." But despite these attempts to introduce new terms, it is the words *chubby* and *chaser* that ultimately seem to endure. The conventional image of the chaser as a "top"—that is, a penetrator—and the chubby as a "bottom"—the one who gets penetrated—is part and parcel of this symbolic structure.

To really understand what is specific about the chubby/chaser pair, however, we can compare the Girth & Mirth scene to another gay male subculture: the Bear scene.[3] The Bear scene is organized by and around men who have particular physical and behavioral attributes. In a roughly hierarchical order, these include facial hair, body hair, manly demeanor, and a confidence with one's physical appearance. Many men who identify as bears are quite heavy. But, contrary to the chubby/chaser scene, size is not the defining feature of membership in the subculture.

The logic of desire is different as well. In Girth & Mirth, desire is aroused because the chubby and chaser are different from each other. Not so in the Bear scene. There, desire is organized not through difference but sameness. The ideal partner for a bearded, hairy, masculine, self-confident bear is another bearded, hairy, masculine, self-confident bear. If a bear couple resembles clones or twins, that is seen as true bliss, and many bears make a lot of effort to look as much alike as they can through coordinated dress and hair/beard styles. The same mirrored logic of attraction also characterizes Bear porn, which usually features a group of versatile men who look more or less identical.

Not so in Girth & Mirth. Chubbies and chasers are rarely confused. They are characterized by their different physiques as well as their different behavior. In the Bear movement, all men are ostensibly the same. In Girth & Mirth, chubbies and chasers tend to take clearly demarcated roles.

Generally speaking, chubs have to "stand there and wait," regardless of whether they are in a gay bar or a virtual chat room. From the chaser's point of view, the sexuality of the chub is immediately apparent. Because the chub is fat, the chaser has the ability to instantly read him as his object of sexual desire.

The chub, by contrast, does not have this kind of option. Chubbies can't assume that the men they see are attracted to them, because they can't be immediately sure that the men are chasers at all. Any educated guess as to the number of chasers among gay men in North America would probably put it at well below 1 percent. Moreover, in an intensely fat-phobic society, there are real strictures against fat people (gay or straight) making sexual advances. Sexual aggressiveness in that context is at best presumptuous, at worst simply ridiculous, a notion constantly reinforced by the representation of fat people as sexual stooges. All this leaves chubs to play the waiting game, hoping to be "picked" by a chaser who might find them attractive.

These dynamics also characterize Convergences in North America. Given the demographic realities of weight in the United States and Canada, chubbies outnumber chasers by a huge margin. At the average event, about five chubbies can be found for every chaser. The result is a microcosm of the despair that sometimes characterizes Girth & Mirth in North America.

Not for the chasers, of course. They are in complete control of the situation. With literally tons of men at their beck and call, they feel and behave like the proverbial "kid in a candy store." Indeed, one could scarcely imagine a more Edenic setting than the one provided by North America's endless supply of ready and willing chubs.

From the perspective of the chubs, the situation looks quite different. They experience the behavior of chasers as one of total entitlement. While they, as chubs, are severely restricted in their actions, chasers can pick and choose. Often this situation leads to genuine hardship. Fleeting encounters may be invested by chubs with emotional depth, and hopes for lasting love become overpowering. As heightened expectations clash with the realities of sexual power, disappointment almost invariably ensues. It does not even take a deliberately abusive chaser—of which many exist as well—to cause devastation. Given the radically different consequences for the two parties, the simple act (or threat) of breaking up, for example, bestows enormous power on a chaser in light of his many options. Chubs, by contrast, often feel that they lack such control. Consequently, they are far more likely to endure bad situations in order to preserve their relationships.

Perhaps this description of the North American chubby/chaser scene is overly dire. It is true, for example, that most chubs experience their initial discovery of Girth & Mirth as a revelation. Having grown up for the most part being continually told that they are unattractive and undesirable, they relish the sexual attention bestowed on them by chasers. Such initial euphoria is often short-lived, however, as chubs gradually discover the inequality and pain built into so much of the chubby/chaser relationship.

A common way of talking about chubbies and chasers in the Girth & Mirth scene, in fact, is to portray chasers as predators and chubbies as their victims. This is a gloomy picture. But it does reflect a reality, characterized by gendered roles and power differentials, of the chubby pining for his Prince Charming and the chaser freely playing the field. Among some members of the scene, this situation has actually prompted a critique that turns on something akin to the chubby's emancipation from the chaser. In practice, this can be observed in some of North America's Girth & Mirth clubs where more and more chubs prefer social and sexual association with other chubs over relationships with chasers, even though they might really be more attracted to slim chasers. This is a strategy that interestingly recalls feminist attempts of the 1970s to achieve sexual and political autonomy through woman-identified sexual object choice.

More recently still, a number of chub-on-chub clubs have been founded, both in major urban centers like New York (Ursus Major) and in cyberspace (the Big Men for Big Men group on Yahoo, for example). For all we know, this kind of chubby solidarity and sex may be the future of Girth & Mirth.

Fat Sex Liberation?

But to return to *Bustin' Apart at the Seams*. It is plausible to see the film, following recent scholarship, as a triumph in the ongoing struggle for fat sexual emancipation. Such a sex-positive perspective links with ideas that emphasize the political potential inherent in alternative sexualities.[4] Much of this position turns on the egalitarian and hence progressive qualities attributed to the sexual communities forged by gay men and lesbians.

But reality is rarely this utopian. As much as a sexual free-for-all might suggest itself as the subversive vehicle of choice, it is hard to enact in the practice of everyday life. The Girth & Mirth scene is merely one example of a sexual field where genuine egalitarianism seems nearly unattainable. More generally, power differentials of size as well as age and race (to name two other obvious instances of inequity) constantly militate against true sexual and political transcendence. It is easy to romanticize the potential of sexual liberation. But in the interest of formulating truly progressive strategies as fat and queer people, we might do better to start with the world as it actually is.

Pissed Off

Allyson Mitchell

We didn't want any old pants. My friends Ruby Rowan and
Mariko Tamaki and I wanted fancy-ass, chunky-butt, nasty-but-
nice, tight-fitting, insanely sexy pants. The three of us were sitting on a park bench, bitching about searching for sexy clothes
that fit. Generally this style of clothing is unavailable to women
of my size. *My size.* At this point in the story you will be wondering what size I am. Well, in truth, my size changes depending on
the brand, quality, scale, and time of the month. Since starting
Pretty Porky and Pissed Off, my weight has fluctuated between
165 pounds and 225 pounds on my five-foot-three-inch frame.

I have been a fat activist for nine years. What I want to recount here is a story of my experiences with the fat activist group called Pretty Porky and Pissed Off. I want to share with you how we fight the Battle of the Bulge from the other side of the fence.

As a plus-size girl, I've always had trouble finding slacks that suit my sassy style. Pants that reflect my *ka-pow* approach to fashion. That spring of 1996, the only pants I could find were school-marmish, elastic-waisted light gray or navy blue depressing pants. On the fateful day of our bitch session on the bench, Ruby said, "Instead of complaining about this, let's do something."

Fat activism is about doing something. It is about changing things. What do we want to change? Just about everything you can think of when it comes to how fat and fat people are treated, thought about, and represented in our society.

The "activism" part of fat activism can range from education and training about body image and eating disorders to reeducation about health and beauty standards. It can include political lobbying to change laws and institutional policies that allow discrimination because of body size. It can be super organized and strategic through organizations like CASA (Canadian Association for Size Acceptance), and, in the U.S., NAAFA (National Association to Advance Size Acceptance), organizations that pressure governments, industries, and advertisers to consider the rights and the dollar power of fat folk. It can be sites of celebration and networking at conferences like "No Lose!" and "Fat Girl Speaks!" Activism can be super social through dances run by organizations like BBW (Big Beautiful Women). It can combine fun and health through events like Fat Girl Yoga or Fat Girl Punk Rock Aerobics Classes. It can be spontaneous and loose through consciousness-raising circles and healthy-cooking teach-ins. It can be healing and proactive like sewing circles where women bring in their "skinny clothes" and sew them into a creative art piece that will hang in strength rather than rest in shame in the back of a closet. It can also include forms of cultural production like performances, Web sites like FED-UP! and even rock bands like The Gossip, with chunky lead singer Beth Ditto. It can be held together by Internet chat communities and textual communities via edited anthologies like Ophira Edut's *Body Outlaws*[1] and zines (self-published writing) like *Fat So!*[2] and *FaT GiRL.*[3]

Mariko, Ruby, and I had heard rumors of girls reclaiming fat, resisting self-loathing, and proclaiming their sex and power in a way that we'd never ever imagined that fat girls could. We found these revolutionaries' voices in self-published zines like Marilyn Wann's *Fat?So!*, Nomy Lamm's *I'm So Fucking Beautiful*, and Sondra Solovay and Max Airborne's *FaT GiRL: A Zine for Fat Dykes and the Women Who Want Them.*[4]

Fanned by these fat flames, Ruby, Mariko, and I started planning.

On a large piece of butcher paper, we scribbled and scrawled until we came up with the perfect name: Pretty Porky and Pissed Off—a group of fed-up fat chicks ready to take on fat phobia, bad body image, and negative fat representations, and to reclaim snacking.

Our name works on several levels. *Pretty* means that fat is not ugly. To many people, fat is sexy, comfortable, comforting, and something to show off, not cover up. *Pretty* is also a relative word: it reflects the fact that all of us in the group are "fairly" fat. We understand that fat comes in more than one size and that its meaning shifts. One person's "small" is another person's "huge" is another person's "chunky" is another person's "svelte." "Fat" is also contingent on race and class. A size-twelve girl at an Ivy League boarding school may be considered fat in the context of white, upper-class body standards. In other circles, age groups, and class situations, a size twelve may be thought of as skinny. Body proportions are different when you consider the body cross-culturally. So a big butt is an asset in some places and a liability in others.

Porky Pig, Blubber, Piglet, Tubby, Fatty Fatty Two-by-Four.

Porky is an ugly word that doesn't have to be.

We use *Porky* in our name in order to rescue a word that is and has been hurled at us (and many fat people) by strangers who see eating in public with a large body as a provocation that deserves humiliation and punishment. Porky is used as a threat and means of exclusion in the playground and at high school dances. We use terms like *Porky* negatively against ourselves every time we look in the mirror and are unable to overcome the messages society sends us if we are fat—messages that, despite our best efforts, infiltrate our own internal monologues: that we are ugly, unworthy, stupid, lazy, and unlovable.

But we are ready to rescue the term and make it our own.

We are ready to come out as porky instead of living in a fat closet.

We've made a conscious choice to live large in the bodies we presently inhabit rather than continue to pretend that we are only temporarily visiting them.

Fat activist Charlotte Cooper addresses this kind of "coming out" in her book *Fat and Proud: The Politics of Size*.[5] She discusses coming out as a fat person as comparable to coming out as gay or lesbian. Rather than trying to make yourself invisible, imagining that you are losing weight, or subscribing to the myth of "the thin person within," Cooper says you can claim a fat identity and stride out into the world as a fat person who is proud.

Regardless of size, all the members of Pretty Porky and Pissed Off are fat. Even when we've dieted ourselves down to 155 pounds, we are still "fat."

"Porky" as a state and not just a word is something that we want to transform because it is something we hate, too, at times. It isn't something you can shake: once you are fat, you are marked in your psyche along with the stretch marks on your skin. You may have the privilege of passing as normal, depending on body size, but there will always be a part of "fat" that stays with you, that informs how you perceive the world and your place in it. Who you are and who you understand yourself to be is shaped by your bodily experiences.

We learn how to move around in the world in a fat psyche.

We are fat regardless of size.

The membership of Pretty Porky and Pissed Off shifts. We lost Ruby to other artistic projects, but gained Abi Slone and Lisa Ayuso. Then we loosened our belts three more notches and added Tracy Tidgwell, Joanne Huffa, and Zoe Whittall. Now we are seven in total, and have been since 2000. As our numbers grew, we formed a kind of a kick-ass girl gang in the city of Toronto. We started dressing to "perform our fat"—to blow it up larger than life.

Sometimes this means extra-tight little cardigans with one trembling button restraining our cleavage.

Sometimes it means wearing teenybopper pop culture fashion like hip-hugger jeans and T-shirts ripped into little tank tops made on our own sewing machines to fit our big childbearing hips and fabulously flabby arms.

Finally, we round our name out with *Pissed Off* because, well, we are. We are pissed off at a culture that tells us we are bad and ugly and unworthy.

We are pissed off at a culture that messed with our heads and told us to eat all this junk food and tempted us constantly with smells and emotions that are meant to addict us chemically and culturally to a high-fat, high-salt diet. This is a culture that tells us to treat ourselves "just this once" over and over again.

It is a culture that harasses us with multibillion-dollar ad campaigns that tell us to be good constant consumers. At the same time, we are punished when our bodies exceed the boundaries of "proper" and "good." It is a culture that tells us be thin at any cost—that thin is the only way to be happy. It is a culture that prays at the diet altar that is proven to not work and in fact makes people ever fatter by screwing with their metabolism and relationship to food and eating.

It is a kajillion-dollar diet and exercise industry in cahoots with mega–food corporations and agribusiness that manufactures boil-in-bag servings that ring in at 500 empty calories and leave us wanting more, both nutritionally and emotionally.

It is a culture that legislates the protection of corporations like Heinz—who owns Weight Watchers, who is in bed with Jenny Craig because they all know that dieting doesn't work, which they also know means that once they get someone started dieting with their products, they essentially get a customer for life.

We will spend so much of our money trying to fulfill our desire to be thin that a good deal of our supposedly "healthy" economy is supported by our fear of getting fat or fatter.

We are pissed off at a culture where, once we are fat (whatever that means—since most people "feel" fat at some point), we are punished for being "gluttons" or "pigs." We are told—and we tell ourselves—that our lack of "control" or "restraint" can be read on our bodies, so we scramble and panic and develop eating disorders to try and escape fat.

As feminists, as women, we feel the brunt of this. What happens to the rules, ideas, and codes about femininity when a bunch of fairly femme-y fat dykes throw around phrases like "Fat and Happy" or "Fat and Proud"? I'll tell you what happens. We smash stereotypes. We explode the ideas that fat women are victims or that girls have to be skinny in order to get a boyfriend or that fat chicks gotta wear muumuus. We are happy and fat—most of the time.

That's why we are Pretty Porky *and* Pissed Off.

Queen-Size Activists

Our first demonstration took place on June 12, 1996. We put out the call to chubby friends and friends of chub. We gathered at the corner of Queen Street West and Soho in downtown Toronto. This area is home to shops that sell the street-smart club wear worn by the teeny-tiny-little-bitty-skirts-and-tops crowd. Most of us lived in the area and felt it was "fitting" that we would be recovering our own neighborhood. We also noted the irony in the name of the street. Queen Street. We were Queen Size! Why couldn't we find clothing to fit us on Queen Street? It seemed to be our right.

We wore tight-fitting crazy outfits, rock-star-diva wear, loud prints, hot pink polyester dresses, and feather boas. We carried signs printed on plastic picnic tablecloths that said FAT!

The demo was a coming out—a proclamation that WE ARE HERE. Look at us and look out. We brought candies to give away and photocopied leaflets about how the average size of women in

Queen size on Queen Street. Courtesy of Jane Farrow

North America is size twelve, yet many Queen Street clothing stores only carry up to size two. We were trying to take the fear out of fat by putting it out on the sidewalk—that same sidewalk we'd walked down in shame, knowing that the only fashions we could purchase in the area were socks, shoes, purses, and barrettes. Those of us who were more timid huddled together in the middle of the group, and those who were feeling more brave approached Sunday shoppers.

We asked them, "Do you think I'm fat?"

The deer-in-the-headlights reaction from shoppers made it clear that they found it shocking that a fat person would ask this question outright. Here we were, actually describing ourselves with the very word we knew was uppermost on the minds of everyone who walked past us. It was as though we were reading their thoughts and saying them out loud—which was clearly scandalous. For many people, the word *fat* is practically unspeakable in polite company.

Here we were, saying the forbidden word in public, taking away its power and sting by saying it first.

Our presence on Queen Street got a lot of media attention. The CBC (Canada's version of NPR) was the first to interview us for a radio documentary. This, in turn, led to an invitation to perform at a gay and lesbian cabaret event called "Cheap Queers." For our first performance, Ruby and I sang a cover song of the reggae hit "Wide Load" but put our political spin its lyrics. We sang, "She's got more rolls than a bakery shop," as if it were a sexy, delicious treat rather than a condemnation. While we sang, Mariko handed out peanut-butter-and-jelly sandwiches and cookies. After our song we pelted the audience with sandwiches. They loved it. Clearly, our fat lesbian bodies had found a place that appealed to women for our feminist messages—and to gay men, too, because we used exaggeration and camp to make some critical points about our culture.

Fat Drag

This performance was the unofficial birth of Pretty Porky and Pissed Off's "fat drag." We call it drag to highlight the made-up nature of fat. Think about how drag queens "perform" femininity. They exaggerate it. They parody it, partly to show how femininity is something constructed, something made up.

This is how we do fat drag.

Think larger than life.

Think bigger and brighter than a Labor Day fireworks display. Not just in size but in color and spirit and comedy.

For our next performance, we used Henry Mancini's "Baby

Elephant Walk" and danced a choreographed routine that we have since performed many times. Lisa, Abi, Mariko, and I—all of various body shapes and proportions—donned traditional dance leotards and walked onstage, carrying perfect and beautiful birthday cakes. We put the cakes on four chairs strategically placed on the stage. Each of us performed our own dance routines highlighting our various plus-size body parts. Lisa featured her ample ass, I emphasized my thick thighs, Mariko and Abi flaunted their bodacious bellies. Then, for the grand finale, we all slowly and teasingly lowered ourselves on the cakes and smushed them with our big fat butts.

Then we all stood up, swiped a fingerful of cake from our soiled leotards, and coyly offered a taste to the audience.

Our Cake Dance is a seemingly innocent and cute performance. However, the politics and effects are very serious. We like to use foods that get particularly fetishized. Buttery, sugary, decadent birthday cakes are a perfect example of this. Over a lifetime, many women develop really unhealthy relationships with foods like this. They want them but deny themselves—then they eat them in secret. Sometimes they vomit them up afterward.

Our Cake Dance is all about having our cake and eating it too.

We now have a repertoire of about ten dances that we use to express our fat politics. We experience powerful emotional effects when we do these types of performances. We often experience a postperformance crash. Putting our bodies out there onstage and using them as tools is exhausting both mentally and physically. In order to get to the point where we are fat activists, it is necessary to consider the pain that caused us to "act" in the first place. The pain of chubby childhoods. The pain of disordered eating. The pain of hating your body for a really long time. The fear of hating our bodies for the rest of our lives.

Our activism is cathartic. I still grieve over the time I've wasted hating my body or torturing it with bulimia or denial or compulsive eating. With this kind of raised consciousness, I feel compelled to try and make as much of a difference as I can—to make up for lost time.

The Double-Edged Sword of the Media

Generally speaking, Pretty Porky and Pissed Off has a sweet relationship with the media. We have been interviewed and appeared on everything from community access cable shows to Internet talk shows to the nationally broadcast news. We have been profiled in university newspapers, glossy magazines alongside Melissa Etheridge, and underground rags and zines. Of course, we always worry about what journalists and others will do with us: Will they hear any of our political criticism? Will they make us look like clowns? (They haven't yet.) We agonize about our words being ignored, twisted, or stupidly contrasted with the opinions of an "expert," inevitably either an eating disorder therapist, a gastric bypass surgeon, or a social worker in a lather about the "obesity epidemic."[6] These stories are always alarmist in tone, and they begin and end with shots of headless unsuspecting fat people shopping or walking down the street. If the fatties are eating an ice cream cone or a candy bar, all the better. These are the bodies meant to represent all the "obese" bodies in North America, the ones who have the "weight problems."

We don't want our bodies to be the ones featured in those kinds of stories.

We don't want to represent that kind of fat—the scary fat that frightens and disgusts people. The sinister fat that lurks behind stories about "Obesity in Newborns." The evil fat that lies behind the "Teenage Girls and Eating Disorder Epidemics." Our whole message is that these kinds of stories promote and spread the very kind of disorders they claim to be combating.

In the end, though, there is no way we can control any of this, and so we have decided to never refuse an interview. We never turn down the opportunity to get our message out to the masses no matter how small or large the masses may be.

While we have sometimes been used as grist for the mill of sensation in the media, most of our coverage has been positive. We've only had one really negative experience. A journalist attacked us in Canada's national newspaper *The Globe and Mail*, saying the message we're spreading is that everyone should be fat, and that the world would be a better place if everybody just took a load off his or her mind and larded up.[7]

This, of course, is not our message. Our message is asserted in the slogans we use, slogans like "Fat Doesn't Necessarily Mean Unhealthy"; "Dieting Makes You Fat"; "Fat Doesn't Mean Lazy"; "Dieting Is Unhealthy And Dangerous"; "Every Body is a Good Body"; and the most outrageous: "Fat Is Sexy."

Most of these messages and slogans are not new to anyone who is familiar with the Fat Liberation Movement, of which we are a part. However, for all those who aren't familiar with Fat Lib, slogans like these may seem threatening and even dangerous.

And in fact, they are.

Marilyn Wann is one of San Francisco's fat revolutionaries. She was one of the people responsible for having size added to the city's code of ethics so that fat people are legally protected from discrimination in hiring and housing. Wann has argued that one reason why people who aren't fat are so hostile toward fat people and fat activism is because they feel, as thin or "normal"-bodied people, that they have sacrificed.[8] They have sacrificed for the bodies they have, and are angry that there are others who don't have the same priorities. I think Wann has a point. It must be infuriating for someone who has spent a lifetime of energy, money, and sacrifice to keep his or her body at a size eight or ten to encounter someone who is just not interested in playing by the same rules. It must be even more enraging to realize that that person actually seems happy.

The unfriendly *Globe and Mail* journalist ended her tirade against us by urging all the members of Pretty Porky and Pissed Off to stop all the nonsense and just lose some weight. That way, she assured us, we'd all be "just as pretty and a lot less pissed off."

With this advice, the journalist put her mean finger on the big fat contradiction that everyone involved in Pretty Porky and Pissed Off embodies in one way or another. While we present as happy, and offer a way of realizing that happiness, many of us—like fat activists everywhere—continue to struggle with different kinds of body complexities. Within our group, we have two histories of eating disorders, and, of course, we all have experienced lifetimes of being told our bodies are wrong. We put on a brave face and do the work. But we also have a number of questions and issues that we discuss continually and for which we have no final answers.

For example, how do we negotiate losing weight while participating in Pretty Porky and Pissed Off? How do we strategize ways to fight fast-food proliferation without sounding fat-phobic? Why are we afraid to perform for teenagers? How do we combat misconceptions that propose that pro-fat means anti-skinny? How can we use our brand of fat activism to fight not only against fat discrimination but also against other power structures like racism and classism?

And then there are the more mundane yet pressing questions, like what should we have for lunch? Contrary to popular stereotypes, fat-ass doesn't equal fast food. The majority of the members of Pretty Porky and Pissed Off are vegetarians. While we do get down with the Krispy Kreme once in a while, we try, like most people, to munch in a balanced way that includes veggies and fruits and other whole foods.

No Big Fat Apologies

It is crucial for fat people to see themselves reflected in art—to see our struggles and our beauty. Dancing together, appearing in public, making speeches, reaching out, performing Cake Dances and sharing experiences with others creates culture and builds communities. When we stop mindlessly consuming culture and begin to actively participate in it, we craft and change our realities. We can imagine alternative ways of living and being.

Like all underground activist groups, we are part of a scene. We do not exist alone. In fact, we are indebted to our active fattie foremothers and dads. We continue to be inspired by the work that goes on around us. Encouraged by legendary fat activists Sondra Solovay and Timnah Steinman, we want our voices and opinions to join others to fight against shame and isolation.

We encourage all fatties to tell their stories.

Ask questions.

Challenge people when they say things that don't sit right in your belly.

Write down your ideas.

Make some new kinds of shopping lists.

Make some demands.

Make the connections.

Do it now.

Photocopy it.

Pass it around.

Post it on the Web.

Perform it.

We can all make art that reflects our bodies and makes our culture see us. Not as fat and ashamed, but as pretty, porky, and pissed off.

Notes

INTRODUCTION

1. Survey of Food, *The Economist*, December 3, 2003, 5–6.

2. Richard Klein, *Eat Fat* (New York: Pantheon Books, 1996), 16.

IDEAL

1. The results of this research are elaborated in Rebecca Popenoe, *Feeding Desire: Fatness and Beauty Among a Saharan People* (London and New York: Routledge, 2003).

2. A recent study by the Ministry of Health in Mauritania found that 11 percent of girls in the country are still force-fed. See Pascale Harter, *Mauritania's "Wife-fattening" Farm*, BBC World News, January 26, 2004, http://news.bbc.co.uk/2/hi/africa/3429903.stm.

3. Sylvia A. Boone, *Radiance from the Waters: Ideals of Feminine Beauty in Mende Art* (New Haven, Conn.: Yale University Press, 1990).

4. Nancy Etcoff, *Survival of the Prettiest: The Science of Beauty* (London: Little, Brown, 1999).

5. Peter J. Brown, "Culture and the Evolution of Obesity," *Human Nature* 2, no. 1 (1991):31–57.

6. Susan Bordo, *Unbearable Weight: Feminism, Western Culture, and the Body* (Berkeley, Calif.: University of California Press, 1993).

7. Naomi Wolf, *The Beauty Myth: How Images of Beauty Are Used Against Women* (New York: Anchor, 1992).

OIL

1. This is Frances Mayes's description of an olive oil tasting from *Under the Tuscan Sun* (New York: Broadway Books, 1997), 204.

2. "Fat Ousts Tobacco as a Threat to Life," *The Toronto Star*, February 11, 2004, A1.

3. Clifford Levy, "The Olive Oil Seems Fine: Whether It's Italian Is the Issue," *The New York Times*, May 7, 2004, www.nytimes.com/2004/05/07/international/europe/07tusc.html. Mort Rosenblum also notes this process in *Olives: The Life and Lore of a Noble Fruit* (New York: Farrar, Straus, Giroux/North Point Press, 1996).

4. Olivier Bausson and Jacques Chibois, *Olive Oil: A Gourmet Guide* (Paris: Flammarion, 2000), 55.

5. Ferenc Mate, *The Hills of Tuscany* (New York: Random House/Delta Books, 1998), 51.

6. *Under the Tuscan Sun*, 203.

7. Alberto Capatti and Massimo Montanari, *Italian Cuisine: A Cultural History* (New York: Columbia University Press, 2003), 71.

8. Clare Ferguson, *Extra Virgin* (New York: Ryland, Peters & Small, 2000), 14.

9. This phrase is inspired by Jane Schneider's class article "Of Vigilance and Virgins," *Ethnology* 3 (1971): 1–24.

10. Lorenza De' Medici, *Lorenza's Pasta* (New York: Clarkson Potter, 1996), 57.

11. *An Oil Called Laudemio* (Florence: Laudemnio Group, 1992), 189.

WHITE

1. Juan Antonio Manya, *Temible Ñakaq?* (Cusco: Allpanchis, 1969), 137.

2. Beth Conklin and Matthew Randall, "Really Alternative Medicine: The Therapeutic Uses of Cannibalism in History and Culture." 10th Annual Philip W. Felts Lecture in the Humanities, Vanderbilt Medical School, April 2004.

3. Manya, 137.

4. Gregorio Condori Mamani and Asunta Quispe Hauman, *Andean Lives: Gregorio Condori Mamani and Asunta Quispe Huaman*, Ricardo Valderrama Fernandez and Carmen Escalante Gutierrez, eds.; Paul H. Gelles and Gabriela Martinez Escobar, trans. (Austin: University of Texas Press, 1996).

5. Peter Gose, "Sacrifice and the Commodity Form in the Andes," *Man* 21 (1994): 296–310. Wachtel cited in Mary Weismantel, *Cholas and Pishtacos: Stories of Race and Sex in the Andes* (Chicago: University of Chicago Press, 2001), 195.

6. Nathan Wachtel, *Gods and Vampires: Return to Chipaya* (originally published in Paris as *Dieux et Vampires: Retour à Chipaya*), Carol Volk, trans. (Chicago: University of Chicago Press, 1994).

7. Juan Ansion and Eudusio Sifuentes, "La Imágen Popular de la Violencia, a traves de los relatos de degolladores," in *Pishtacos: De Verdugos a Sacaojos*, Juan Ansion, ed. (Lima: Tarea, Asociacion de Publicaciones Educativas, 1989).

8. Enrique Mayer, "Patterns of Violence in the Andes," *Latin American Research Review* 29, no. 2, 141–177.

9. Ibid., 104.

PHAT

1. Big Pun, *Yeeeah Baby*, Introduction (Loud Records, CK63843, 2000).

2. Marcos Antonio Miranda and Liza Ríos (2002). *Still Not a Player*, Miranda Movies, DVD (2002).

3. Ibid.

4. Big Pun, "Brave in the Heart," *Endangered Species* (Loud Records, REK-11963, 2001).

5. It is interesting that the most famous white gangsta rapper has taken the name Slim Shady, further coalescing whiteness with thinness.

6. Sohnya Sayres, "Glory Mongering: Food and the Agon of Excess," *Social Text* 16 (Winter 1986–87).

7. Miranda and Ríos.

8. Ibid.

9. Patrick Atoon, "The Rap Dictionary" (Sept. 15, 2002), www.rapdict.org/terms/

10. Mimi Nichter, *Fat Talk: What Girls and Their Parents Say About Dieting* (Cambridge, Mass.: Harvard University, 2000), 163–180.

11. Sir Mix-a-Lot, *Baby Got Back* (American Recordings, 093624023326, 1992).

12. In Nichter, 179.

13. According to CDC statistics, African American adult women have the highest rate of obesity, a remarkable 50 percent. Centers for Disease Control, National Center for Health Statistics, Dec. 24, 2002, www.cdc.gov/nchs/releases/02news/obesityonrise.htm.

14. Laura Kipnis points out that almost 30 percent of women with incomes below $10,000 are obese as compared to 12.7 percent of those with incomes over

$50,000. Laura Kipnis "Fat and Culture," in Nicholas Dirks, ed., *Near Ruins: Cultural Theory at the End of the Century* (Minneapolis: University of Minnesota Press, 1998), 206.

15. Adam Drenowski and S. E. Specter, "Poverty and Obesity: The Role of Energy Density and Energy Costs," *American Journal of Clinical Nutrition* 79: 6–16.

16. Kipnis, 206–207.

17. St. Lunatics, "Jang A Lang," *Free City* (Universal Records, 440 014 119-a, 2001).

18. The average fashion model today weighs 23 percent less than the average woman. A generation ago the gap was only 8 percent. Cecilia Hartley, "Letting Ourselves Go: Making Room for the Fat Body in Feminist Scholarship," in Jana Evans Braziel and Kathleen LeBesco, eds. *Bodies Out of Bounds* (Berkeley: University of California Press, 2000), 61.

19. www.mtv.com/news/articles/1484248/20040109/story.jhtml.

20. www.mtv.com/news/articles/1428938/19990304/story.jhtml.

21. Fat Joe, "The Hidden Hand," *Don Cartagena* (Atlantic, 1998).

22. Big Pun, "I Ain't a Player," *Capital Punishment* (RCA 67648-2, 1998).

23. Fat Joe, "What's Love," *Jealous Ones Still Envy* (Atlantic, 83472-2, 2001).

24. Jerry Mosher, "Setting Free the Bears: Refiguring Fat Men on Television," in Jana Evans Braziel and Kathleen LeBesco, eds., *Bodies Out of Bounds* (Berkeley: University of California Press, 2001), 170.

25. "I ain't a player, I just fuck a lot. Jump on top of my dick and work them hips until I bust a shot." Big Pun, "I Ain't a Player," *Capital Punishment* (RCA, 67648-2, 1998).

26. Miranda and Ríos.

27. Ibid.

28. Big Pun, "Boomerang," *Capital Punishment* (RCA, 67648-2, 1998).

29. Notorious B.I.G., "I Got a Story to Tell," *Ready to Die* (Bad Boy, 1994).

30. Heavy D, "Buncha Niggas," *Blue Funk* (MCA, 1992).

31. Big Pun, "Wrong Ones," *Yeeeah Baby* (Loud Records, CK63843, 2000).

32. Big Pun, "Parental Discretion," *Capital Punishment* (RCA, 67648-2, 1998).

33. Hillel Schwartz, *Never Satisfied: A Cultural History of Diets, Fantasies and Fat* (New York: Free Press, 1986).

34. Mosher, 177.

PORN

1. Johnny Maldoro, "Where the fat women at!" *The Village Voice*, October 2–8, 2002, 236.

2. See for example, www.bigcuties.com. I am extremely grateful to Heather Boyle, the owner of this Web site, for her generosity in providing me with images to illustrate this essay. I encourage anyone who is interested to visit her Web site.

3. www.zaftig-2000.com/russo/, last checked in November 2003.

4. www.supersizebbw.com, last checked in May 2003. In late 2003, Betsy decided to retire from the business and pursue other interests, such as writing. She has already published a book for children about size discrimination. Her new Web site is www.bbwsanctuary.com. (I am grateful to Fuchsia at Bountiful Productions for this update.)

5. *FaT GiRL* (San Francisco: FaT GiRL Publishing, 1994).

6. Ibid., no. 2, 2.

7. Katharine Gates, *Deviant Desires: Incredibly Strange Sex* (New York: Juno Books and RE/Search, 2000), 199.

8. Ibid.

9. *FaT GiRL*, no. 3, 43.

10. Mimi Nichter, *Fat Talk: What Girls and Their Parents Say About Dieting* (London: Harvard University Press, 2000). See also the chapter titled "Phat" in this book.

11. *FaT GiRL*, no. 1, 2.

12. Laura Kipnis, *Bound and Gagged: Pornography and the Politics of Fantasy in America* (Durham, N.C.: Duke University Press, 1999), 121.

13. Many thanks to Max Airborne for obtaining permission to use this image.

14. Linda Williams, *Hard Core: Power, Pleasure, and the "Frenzy of the Visible"* (Berkeley and Los Angeles: University of California Press, 1999), xvi.

HEAVENLY

1. Vila Branca is a pseudonym employed to protect the privacy of the people I discuss. I have written about Vila Branca and its inhabitants in much more detail in my book *Feminine Matters: Women's Religious Practices in a Portuguese Town* (Stockholm: Almqvist & Wiksell, 2000).

2. Joao de Pina-Cabral, *Sons of Adam, Daughters of Eve: The Peasant Worldview of the Alto Minho* (Oxford, U.K.: Clarendon Press, 1986).

3. The biographical data on Alexandrina are found in Humberto Pascoal, *Sob o Céu de Balasar* (Porto, Portugal: Edicões Salesianas and Gabriele Amorth, 1983), and Humberto Pascoal, *Por Detrás de um Sorriso: Alexandrina Maria da Costa* (Porto, Portugal: Edicões Salesianas, 1992).

4. Caroline Bynum, *Holy Feast and Holy Fast: The Religious Significance of Food to Medieval Women* (Berkeley: University of California Press, 1987), and Grace Jantzen, *Power, Gender and Christian Mysticism* (Cambridge: Cambridge University Press, 1995).

5. Bynum, 73.

6. Jantzen.

7. Catherine Wessinger, "Ordination: In Christianity," in S. Young, ed. *Encyclopaedia of Women and World Religion* (New York: Macmillan Reference USA, 1999), 743.

TALK

1. A few examples in English and Swedish are: Carita Bengs, *Looking Good. A Study of Gendered Body Ideals Among Young People* (Umeå, Sweden: Umeå University Press, 2000); Nina Björk, *Under Det Rosa Täcket: Om Kvinnlighetens Vara och Feministiska Strategier* (Copenhagen: Wahlström & Widstrand, 1996); Susan Bordo, *Unbearable Weight: Feminism, Western Culture and the Body* (Berkeley: University of California Press, 1993); Jorun Solheim, *Den Öppna Kroppen: Om Könssymbolik i Modern Kultur* (Uddevalla, Sweden: Daidalos, 2001); and Naomi Wolf, *The Beauty Myth: How Images of Beauty Are Used Against Women* (New York: Anchor Books, 2001).

2. Wolf, *The Beauty Myth*, 183.

3. Pierre Bourdieu and Loïq Wacquant, *Invitation to a Reflexive Sociology* (Chicago: University of Chicago Press, 1991).

4. Mimi Nichter, *Fat Talk: What Girls and Their Parents Say About Dieting* (Cambridge, Mass.: Harvard University Press, 2000).

LEAKY

1. Survey of Food, *The Economist*, December 3, 2003, 4, 9.

2. World Bank, *World Development Indicators: Distribution of Income or Consumption* (2002).

3. Barbara Ehrenreich, *Fear of Falling: The Inner Life of the Middle Class* (New York: Harper Perennial, 1990) and U.S. Census Bureau, *Current Population Survey* (2000).

4. E. P. Reis, "Modernization, Citizenship and Stratification: Historical Processes and Recent Changes in Brazil," in *Daedalus* 129, no. 2, 171–194; C. H. Wood and J.A.M. Carvalho, *The Demography of Inequality in Brazil* (New York: Cambridge University Press, 1988); and R. Schneider, *Brazil: Culture and Politics in a New Industrial Powerhouse* (Boulder, Colo.: Westview Press, 1996).

5. *Síntese de Indicadores Sociais* (IBGE: 2002); and R. Schneider, Ibid.

6. Roberto DaMatta, *Carnavais, Malandros e Heróis* (Rio de Janeiro: Zahar, 1978).

7. M. O'Dougherty, *Consumption Intensified: The Politics of Middle-Class Life in Brazil* (Durham, N.C.: Duke University Press, 2002).

8. "Model is remade for *Playboy* as Brazil goes under the scalpel," *The Guardian* 29, November 2000.

9. According to the Brazilian Association of Plastic Surgery (in *Veja*, "Corpos à venda," March 6, 2002). American Society for Aesthetic Plastic Surgery, *2001 Statistics*.

10. L. Bethell, "Politics in Brazil: From Elections without Democracy to Democracy without Citizenship," *Daedalus* 129, no. 2, 1–28.

11. "Publishing in Brazil: Is the glass half empty or half full?" FIPP (Fédération Internationale de la Presse Périodique) *Magazine World*, quarter 3 (2003), no. 38, www.fipp.com/1125.

12. "Brazilians queue for new breasts before carnival," www.telegraph.co.uk/news, January 21, 2001.

13. "Unnatural Beauty: Miss Brazil Boasts 19 Procedures," abcnews.com, May 3, 2001.

14. Don Kulick, *Travesti: Sex, Gender and Culture Among Brazilian Transgendered Prostitutes* (Chicago: University of Chicago Press, 1998).

15. "Unnatural Beauty: Miss Brazil Boasts 19 Procedures," abcnews.com, May 3, 2001.

16. R. W. Fogel, *Without Consent or Contract: The Rise and Fall of American Slavery* (New York and London: W. W. Norton & Company, 1989).

17. For more on this commercial and Brazilian media, see Thaïs Machado-Borges, *Only for You! Brazilians and the Telenovela Flow* (Stockholm: Almqvist & Wiksell, 2003).

LARD

1. Anthropologist Alison Leitch has written about a similar struggle in Carrara, Italy. See Alison Leitch, "Slow Food and the Politics of Pork Fat: Italian Food and European Identity," *Ethnos* 28 (2003), no. 4, 437–62.

2. Leitch (2003) also describes how *lardo di Colonnata* has been championed by the Slow Food movement, an international organization dedicated to preserving local foods and their "slow" enjoyment, in contrast to the tastes and consumption practices characteristic of fast food.

3. Polly Weissner, "Introduction: Food, Status, Culture, and Nature," in *Food and the Status Quest: An Interdisciplinary Perspective*, Polly Weissner & Wulf Schiefenhövel, eds. (Providence, R.I.: Berghahn Books, 1996), 1–23.

INDULGENCE

1. "Seattle in a froth over latte tax," *The Guardian*, August 19, 2003.

2. *Seattle Times*, September 17, 2003.

3. William Roseberry, "The Rise of Yuppie Coffees and the Reimagination of Class in the United States," *American Anthropologist* 98, 762–775.

4. Ibid.

5. Cited in Joanne Finkelstein, "Dining Out: The Hyperreality of Appetite," in Ron Scapp and Brian Seilz, eds., *Eating Culture* (Albany, N.Y.: State University of New York Press, 1998), 216.

6. *Nutrition Action Healthletter*, July/August 2004. Center for Science in the Public Interest Web site.

7. *Nutrition Action Healthletter*, October 2002. Center for Science in the Public Interest Web site.

8. According to the CSPI, although the Crème Frappuccinos are the highest-calorie drinks Starbucks sells, two other drinks actually have more saturated fat—the Chocolate Brownie Frappuccino and the Mocha Coconut Frappuccino each have 23 grams of saturated fat—considered by the CSPI as more than a day's worth of fat. The original article can be found at www.cspinet.org/new/200210072.html.

9. www.dwlz.com/Restaurants/starbucks.html.

10. *Nutrition Action Healthletter*, July/August 2004. Center for Science in the Public Interest Web site.

11. C. Esselstyn, American Association of Endocrine Surgeons Presidential Address: "Beyond Surgery," April 1998.

12. Richard Hooker, *Food and Drink in America: A History* (New York: Bobbs-Merrill, 1981), 61–62.

13. *Foods, Fats and Oils* New York, Institute of Shortening and Edible Oils, 1999.

14. Judy Puman, Jane Allshouse, and Linda Scott Kantor, "U.S. Per Capita Food Supply Trends: More Calories, Refined Carbohydrates, and Fats," *Food Review* 25, no. 3 (1992):15.

15. Ibid., 6–7.

16. Sidney Mintz, *Tasting Food, Tasting Freedom: Excursions into Eating, Culture and the Past* (Boston: Beacon Press, 1996).

17. Ibid., 118.

18. Jane Dusselier, "Bonbons, Lemon Drops and Oh Henry! Bars: Candy, Consumer Culture and the Construction of Gender, 1895–1920," in Sherrie Inness, ed., *Kitchen Culture in America: Popular Representations of Food, Gender and Race* (Philadelphia: University of Pennsylvania Press, 2001), 95–118.

CHAOS

1. Steven Kruger, "'GET FAT, don't die!' Eating and AIDS in Gay Men's Culture," in Ron Scapp and Brian Seitz, eds., *Eating Culture* (Albany: State University of New York Press, 1998), 40.

2. Ibid., 51.

SPAM

1. Ann Kondo Corum, *Hawai'i's Spam Cookbook* (Honolulu: The Bess Press, 1987), xv.

2. www.spam.com. Last visited May 31, 2004.

3. Rachel Laudan, *The Food of Paradise: Exploring Hawai'i's Culinary Heritage* (Honolulu: University of Hawai'i Press, 1996).

4. www.detritus.org/spam/skit.html.

5. www.home.hawaii.rr.com/huckster/hawaii/living3.html. Last visited May 20, 2004.

6. Laudan.

7. John Casken, "Improved Health Status for Native Hawaiians: Not Just What the Doctor Ordered," *Wicazo* (Spring, 2000):75.

8. www.kbeamer.com/spam_haiku.html. Visited May 31, 2004.

9. www.bizjournals.com/pacific/stories/2003/04/07/smallb2.html. Visited May 31, 2004.

10. E.g., Laura Kipnis, *Bound and Gagged: Pornography and the Politics of Fantasy in America* (New York: Grove Press, 1996), 100.

11. An Interview with Mililani Trask, *He Alo A He Alo* Face to Face: Hawaiian Voices on Sovereignty, 123. Edited by Roger MacPherson Farrar (Honolulu: American Friends Service Committee—Hawai'i, 1993).

12. Sidney Mintz, *Sweetness and Power: The Place of Sugar in Modern History* (New York: Penguin Books, 1986).

13. Peter Stearns, *Fat History: Bodies and Beauty in the Modern West* (New York: New York University Press, 1997), 137.

CHASERS

1. Laura Kipnis, *Bound and Gagged: Pornography and the Politics of Fantasy in America* (New York: Grove, 1996), 94.

2. Ibid., 114. See also Richard Klein, *Eat Fat* (New York: Pantheon Books, 1996) and Jana Evans Braziel and Kathleen LeBesco, eds., *Bodies Out of Bounds: Fatness and Transgression* (Berkeley: University of California Press, 2001).

3. On the Bear movement, see Les Wright, ed., *The Bear Book: Readings in the History and Evolution of a Gay Male Subculture* (New York: Harrington Press, 1997); Les Wright, ed., *The Bear Book II: Further Readings in the History and Evolution of a Gay Male Subculture* (New York: Harrington Press, 2001); and Ron Suresha, *Bears on Bears: Interviews and Discussions* (Los Angeles: Alyson Books, 2002).

4. Michael Warner, *The Trouble with Normal: Sex, Politics, and the Ethics of Queer Life* (New York: Free Press, 1999); Michael Warner, *Publics and Counterpublics* (New York: Zone Books, 2002), especially Chapter 5 (cowritten with Lauren Berlant), "Sex in Public," 187–208; and David Halperin, *Saint Foucault: Towards a Gay Hagiography* (New York: Oxford University Press, 1995).

PISSED OFF

1. Ophira Edut, ed., *Body Outlaws: Young Women Write About Body Image and Identity* (New York: Seal Press, 2000).

2. Marilyn Wann, *Fat?So! Zine: For People Who Don't Apologize For Their Size* (San Francisco: self-published, 1995–2004).

3. Sondra Solovay and Max Airborne, eds., *FaT GiRL* (San Francisco: FaT GiRL Publishing, 1994–1997).

4. Nomy Lamm, *I'm So Fucking Beautiful* (self-published, 1993–96).

5. Charlotte Cooper, *Fat and Proud: The Politics of Size* (London: Women's Press, 1998).

6. Paul Campos, author of *The Obesity Myth* (New York: Penguin Putnam, 2004), argues that North Americans' obsession with obesity is more a myth or a moral panic than a real epidemic.

7. Leah McLaren, "Porky Pride? Fat Lot of Good That Will Do," *The Globe and Mail*, Saturday, February 12, 2000.

8. Wann.

Acknowledgments

We are especially grateful to two people: our agent, Douglas Stewart, was enthusiastic about this project from the start, and his support and guidance have been invaluable. Our editor at Tarcher, Ashley Shelby, has been remarkable. Her input has been substantial: it has been instrumental in crafting, focusing, and polishing every chapter in this book.

Don would also like to thank Christine Heycke, Christopher Stroud, and Jonas Tillberg for their comments on drafts of various proposals and chapters. I also gratefully acknowledge the support of the Bank of Sweden Tercentenary Foundation for a research grant that enabled some of the time spent preparing this book.

Anne wants to thank her colleagues and dear friends Bruce Grant, Deborah Heath, Michael Levin, Paul Manning, and Donna Young. None of them was directly involved in this project but all were wonderfully supportive at every stage. I appreciate the enthusiasm of the Banelis, Bersenas, and Meneley clans, especially Vaidila and Theo Banelis, who lived most immediately with the ups and downs of the volume. A special thanks to Jane and Margie Zeidler for putting us in touch with Allyson Mitchell.

Contributors

FANNY AMBJÖRNSSON is an anthropologist at the Center for Gender Studies, Stockholm University, Sweden. She has coauthored two books: *Ett Hjärta i Jeans* (*A Heart in Jeans*, Alfabeta, 1997), about teenage girls, and *Uppror Pågår* (*Rebellion Happens*, Alfabeta, 1999), which is a history of feminism for teenagers. Her book *I en Klass för Sig* (*In a Class of Their Own*), about gender and sexuality among high school girls, was published by Ordfront Publishers in 2004.

MATTI BUNZL is associate professor of anthropology at the University of Illinois at Urbana-Champaign, where he also directs the Illinois Program for Research in the Humanities. His book *Symptoms of Modernity: Jews and Queers in Late-Twentieth Century Vienna* was published in 2004 by the University of California

Press. He has coedited the anthology *Altering States: Ethnographies of Transition in Eastern Europe and the Former Soviet Union* (University of Michigan Press, 2000) and has published articles on gay sex, tourism, coffee houses, and gay slang.

JILLIAN R. CAVANAUGH is assistant professor at the Department of Anthropology, Brooklyn College, CUNY. She has published articles on linguistic and cultural preservation in Bergamo, Italy.

LENA GEMZÖE is an anthropologist based at the Center for Gender Studies, Stockholm University, Sweden. She has published a Swedish introduction to feminist theory, *Feminism* (Bilda Förlag, 2002), and *Feminine Matters: Women's Religious Practices in a Portuguese Town* (Almqvist & Wiksell, 2000), a study that interprets how and why women participate in the Catholic religion.

MARK GRAHAM is associate professor at the Department of Social Anthropology, Stockholm University, Sweden. He has published articles on topics as diverse as the Swedish labor market, masculinity and embodiment, gay male leather culture, the Internet, sexuality and consumption, queer theory, and tourism.

JOAN GROSS is professor of anthropology at Oregon State University. She is the author of *Speaking in Other Voices: An Ethnography of Walloon Puppet Theaters* (John Benjamins, 2001). She has also published numerous articles on minority languages and popular music in Europe and the United States.

JULIA HARRISON is associate professor of anthropology and chair of women's studies at Trent University, Canada. Her recent book, *Being a Tourist: Finding Meaning in Pleasure Travel* (University of British Columbia Press, 2003), examines the travel narratives of upper-middle-class Canadian tourists.

THAÏS MACHADO-BORGES is a researcher at the Department of Social Anthropology, Stockholm University, Sweden. She is the author of *Only for You! Brazilians and the Telenovela Flow* (Almqvist & Wiksell, 2003).

ALLYSON MITCHELL is a maximalist visual artist who creates images of sexy fat women with craft, fun fur, and collections of found objects. Her filmography of twenty works includes titles like *Chow Down*, *Candy Kisses*, and *Foodie*. In her spare time, she teaches feminist activism at York University, Canada, and works on her dissertation about women, power, and space. For more information, go to www.AllysonMitchell.ca.

REBECCA POPENOE is a visiting lecturer in anthropology at Uppsala University, Sweden. Her book, *Feeding Desire: Fatness, Beauty, and Sexuality Among a Saharan People*, was published by Routledge in 2003. She has published articles on body modification, beauty, sexuality, and health and illness.

MARY WEISMANTEL is professor of anthropology and director of Latin American and Caribbean studies at Northwestern University. Food, death, sex, and race are among her scholarly interests; she has been researching these topics in the Andes Mountains of South America since 1985. She has published two books, *Cholas and Pishtacos: Tales of Race and Sex in the Andes* (University of Chicago Press, 2001) and *Food, Gender, and Poverty in the Ecuadorian Andes* (University of Pennsylvania Press, 1988; reprinted in 1998 by Westview Press).

MARGARET WILLSON is an anthropologist and codirector of Bahia Street, a social justice agency that works primarily in Brazil. She is coeditor, with Don Kulick, of the book *Taboo: Sex, Gender, and Erotic Subjectivity in Anthropological Fieldwork* (Routledge, 1995), and has written articles in scholarly journals and popular magazines on topics such as opium smuggling, mountaineering, Chinese trading in the Pacific, and the Brazilian martial art *capoeira*.

About the Editors

DON KULICK is a professor of anthropology at New York University. He has written and edited numerous books and articles, both scholarly and popular, in both English and Swedish. His most recent book is *Language and Sexuality*, was coauthored with Deborah Cameron and published in 2003 by Cambridge University Press. His anthropological works include *Language Shift and Cultural Reproduction: Socialization, Syncretism and Self in a Papua New Guinean Village* (Cambridge University Press, 1992) and *Travesti: Sex, Gender and Culture Among Brazilian Transgendered Prostitutes* (University of Chicago Press, 1998).

ANNE MENELEY is an associate professor of anthropology at Trent University, Canada. She is the author of *Tournaments of Value: Sociability and Hierarchy in a Yemeni Town* (University of Toronto

Press, 1996), and has published articles about Yemen, as well as about her research on the production, circulation, and consumption of Tuscan extra-virgin olive oil. Her most recent work, coedited with Donna Young, is entitled *Auto-Ethnographies of the Academy* (Broadview, 2005). The book explores the bizarre and recondite aspects of academic labor.

Credits